mini atlas

Bartholomew

Edinburgh

1971

© John Bartholomew & Son Ltd., Edinburgh
Printed and Published in Great Britain by
John Bartholomew & Son Ltd. 1971
SBN   85152 804 X

Contents

Contents

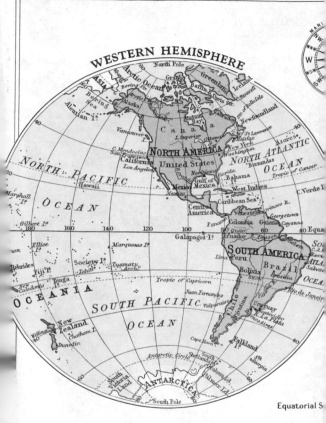

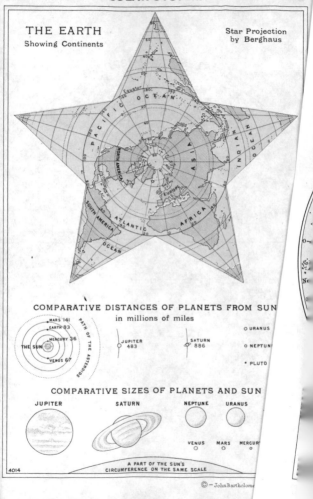

THE EARTH
Showing Continents

Star Projection
by Berghaus

COMPARATIVE DISTANCES OF PLANETS FROM SUN
in millions of miles

MARS 141
EARTH 93
MERCURY 36
THE SUN
VENUS 67
PATH OF THE ASTEROIDS

JUPITER
483

SATURN
886

O URANUS

O NEPTUN

* PLUTO

COMPARATIVE SIZES OF PLANETS AND SUN

JUPITER

SATURN

NEPTUNE

URANUS

VENUS   MARS   MERCURY

A PART OF THE SUN'S
CIRCUMFERENCE ON THE SAME SCALE

4014

© — John Bartholomew

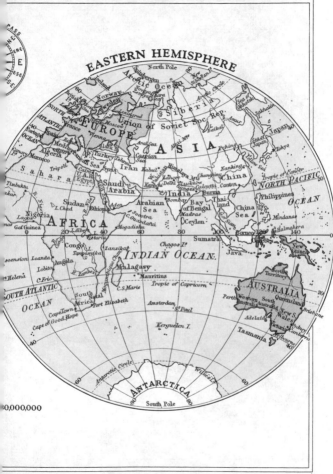

EASTERN HEMISPHERE

North Pole
Arctic Ocean
Arctic Circle
Spitzbergen
New Siberian Is.
Sea of Okhotsk
Sakhalin
Iceland
Novaya Zemlya
Norway
Sweden
Siberia
Amur
Japan
Sea of Japan
Tokyo
Moscow
Union of Soviet Soc. Rep.
Baikal
EUROPE
France
Spain
Black Sea
Aral Sea
Caspian Sea
ASIA
Peking
Yellow Sea
NORTH ATLANTIC OCEAN
Italy
Mediterranean Sea
Turkey
Tehran
Iran
Kabul
Himalayas
Nanking
China
Tropic of Cancer
NORTH PACIFIC OCEAN
Azores
Morocco
Algeria
Tripoli
Cairo
U.A.R.
Egypt
Syria
Iraq
Saudi Arabia
Karachi
Lahore
Lucknow
Chungking
Canton
Delhi
Sahara
Timbuktu
Dakar
Sudan
Nile
Aden
Arabian Sea
Bombay
India
Ganges
Calcutta
Madras
Burma
Thailand
Siam
China Sea
Philippines
Mindanao
Halmahera
Nigeria
Lagos
G. of Guinea
Ethiopia
Socotra
Ceylon
AFRICA
Congo
Victoria L.
Mogadishu
C. Guardafui
Sumatra
Borneo
Celebes
New Guinea
Ascension
Loanda
Angola
Lobito
R. Zambezi
Tanganyika
Zanzibar
Chagos Is.
INDIAN OCEAN
Java
St. Helena
C. Frio
Malagasy
Mauritius
Territory
AUSTRALIA
Queensland
SOUTH ATLANTIC OCEAN
South Africa
Port Elizabeth
C. S. Marie
Tropic of Capricorn
Perth
Western Australia
South Australia
New South Wales
Brisbane
Sydney
Cape Town
Cape of Good Hope
Amsterdam
St. Paul
Adelaide
Victoria
Melbourne
Kerguelen I.
Tasmania
Antarctic Circle
Wilkes Ld.
ANTARCTICA
South Pole

:80,000,000

© – John Bartholomew & Son. Ltd. Edinburgh.

4

RELIEF

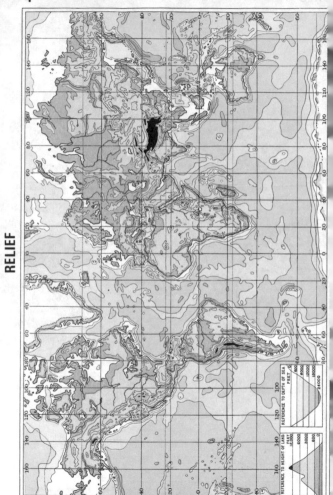

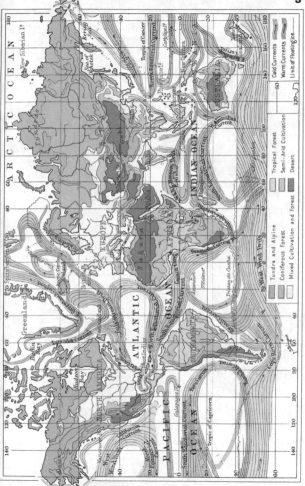

5

© John Bartholomew & Son, Ltd. Edinburgh.

6

TEMPERATURE—JANUARY

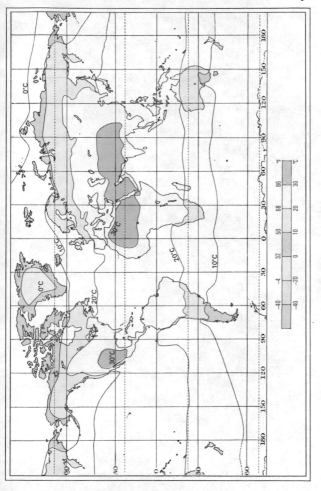

COMMUNICATIONS

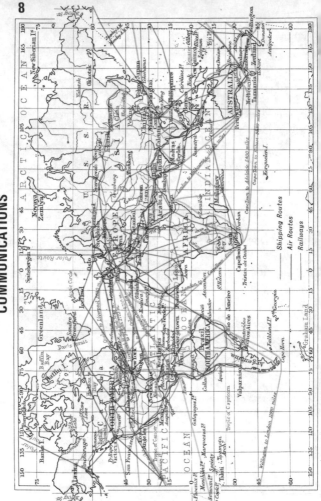

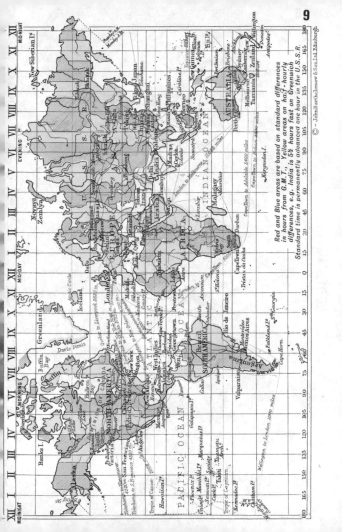

Red and Blue areas are based on standard differences in hours from G.M.T., Yellow areas on half-hourly differences, e.g. India is 5½ hours fast on Greenwich Standard time is permanently advanced one hour in the U.S.S.R.

© — John Bartholomew & Son, Ltd. Edinburgh.

NORTH AMERICA

ATLAN

UNITED STATES

MEXICO

SOUTH AMERICA

CENTRAL AMERICA

WEST INDIES

GULF OF MEXICO

CARIBBEAN SEA

Bahama Islands

CUBA

JAMAICA

HONDURAS

GUATEMALA

NICARAGUA

Florida

Bermudas

New York
Philadelphia
Pittsburg
Washington
Baltimore
Richmond
Raleigh
C. Hatteras
Charleston
Savannah
Jacksonville
C. Sable

Cincinnati
Louisville
Atlanta
Montgomery
Mobile
New Orleans
Memphis
Nashville
Vicksburg

St. Louis
Chicago
Indianapolis
Kansas City
Omaha
Des Moines

Denver
Santa Fé
Albuquerque
El Paso
Little Rock
Dallas
Austin
Galveston
Brownsville

Havana
C. Catoche
Yucatan
G. of Campeche
Vera Cruz
Tampico
C. Rojo
Orizaba

Monterey
Zacatecas
Guanajuato
León
Guadalajara
Popocatepetl
ACAPULCO
MEXICO

Sierra Madre

Rio Grande
Chihuahua

Gulf of California
Lower California
C. Corrientes
Mazatlan
C. S. Lucas
Socorro I.
Guadalupe

Tropic of Cancer

San Francisco
Sacramento
Sierra Nevada
Carson City
Los Angeles
San Diego
Mt. Whitney
Salt Lake
Great Salt Lake
Pikes Peak

Panama Canal
Colon
Panama

Missouri R.
Platte R.
Colorado R.
Red R.
Ohio R.
Mississippi

PACIFIC OCEAN

Statute Miles
0 100 200 300 400 500   1000

30

20

10

70

80

90

100

110

120

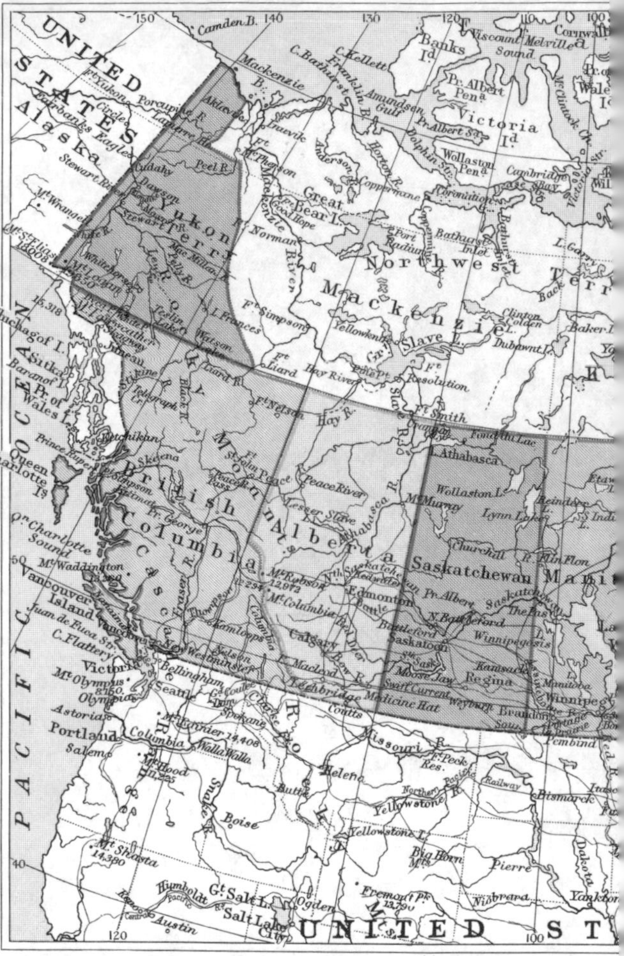

UNITED STATES
Alaska
Yukon Terr.
British Columbia
Alberta
Saskatchewan
Northwest Terr.
Mackenzie
PACIFIC OCEAN
UNITED STATES
Camden B.
Mackenzie B.
C. Bathurst
C. Kellett
Franklin B.
Amundsen Gulf
Banks Id.
Viscount Melville Sound
Pr. Albert Pena.
Victoria Id.
Pr. Albert Sd.
Wollaston Pena.
Dolphin Str.
Cambridge Bay
Coronation G.
M'Clintock Ch.
Aklavik
Inuvik
Ft. McPherson
Ft. Yukon
Porcupine R.
Circle
Fairbanks
Eagle
Peel R.
Dawson
Stewart R.
Mt. Wrangell
White R.
Mt. St. Elias 18008
Mt. Logan 19850
Whitehorse
Mac Millan R.
Pelly R.
Teslin L.
L. Frances
Watson Lake
Great Bear L.
Ft. Good Hope
Ft. Norman
Mackenzie River
Port Radium
Bathurst Inlet
Anderson R.
Horton R.
Coppermine
Coppermine R.
Ft. Simpson
Yellowknife
Gr. Slave L.
Ft. Resolution
Ft. Liard
Liard R.
Hay River
Pine Pt.
Slave R.
Ft. Smith
Ft. Nelson
Hay R.
Clinton Colden L.
Dubawnt L.
Baker L.
Back R.
L. Garry
Chichagof I.
Sitka
Baranof I.
Juneau
Skagway
Stikine R.
Telegraph Cr.
Black R.
Pr. of Wales I.
Ketchikan
Prince Rupert
Skeena
Queen Charlotte Is.
Qn. Charlotte Sound
Ft. St. John
Peace R.
Peace River
Lesser Slave L.
Athabasca R.
Ft. McMurray
L. Athabasca
Fond du Lac
Wollaston L.
Lynn Lake
Reindeer L.
Churchill
Flin Flon
Pr. George
Mt. Robson 12,972
Mt. Columbia
Mt. Waddington 13,260
Vancouver Island
Nanaimo
Vancouver
New Westminster
Juan de Fuca Str.
C. Flattery
Victoria
Kamloops
Thompson
Fraser R.
Columbia R.
Nelson
Edmonton
Red Deer
Calgary
Bow R.
Lethbridge
Medicine Hat
Coutts
Swift Current
Moose Jaw
Regina
Weyburn
Saskatoon
Battleford
N. Battleford
Pr. Albert
The Pas
Winnipegosis
Kamsack
Brandon
Winnipeg
L. Manitoba
Portage la Prairie
Pembina
Bellingham
Seattle
Mt. Olympus 8,150
Olympia
Astoria
Portland
Salem
Mt. Hood 11,225
Mt. Rainier 14,408
Spokane
Walla Walla
Snake R.
Missouri R.
Ft. Peck Res.
Helena
Butte
Northern Pacific Railway
Bismarck
Yellowstone R.
Yellowstone L.
Boise
Big Horn Mts.
Pierre
Dakota
Yankton
Niobrara
Mt. Shasta 14,380
Humboldt
Reno
Austin
Gt. Salt L.
Ogden
Salt Lake City
Fremont Pk. 13,790
150
140
130
120
110
100
50
40

Statute Miles

0   100   200   300   400

GREENLAND

ATLANTIC

Baffin Bay

Baffin Id.

Davis Strait

Hudson Str.

Hudson Bay

James Bay

Labrador

Peninsula

Newfoundland

Gulf of St.Lawrence

Cape Breton I.

OCEAN

Quebec

Ontario

New Brunswick

Nova Scotia

L. Superior

L. Michigan

L. Huron

L. Erie

L. Ontario

OTTAWA

Montreal

Toronto

Quebec

Buffalo

Detroit

Cleveland

Pittsburgh

NEW YORK

Boston

Cape Cod

Halifax

C. Sable

© John Bartholomew & Son, Ltd. Edinburgh

WESTERN PROVINCES

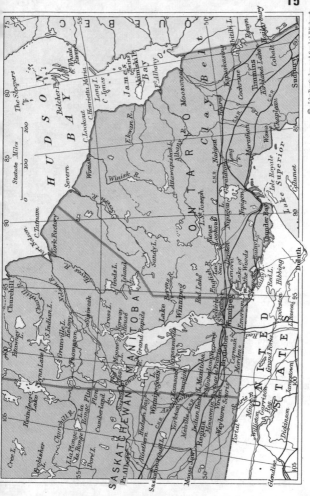

© John Bartholomew & Son, Ltd. Edinburgh.

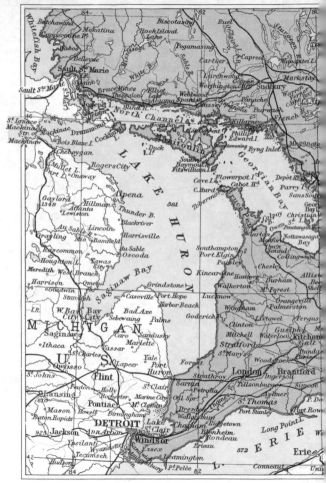

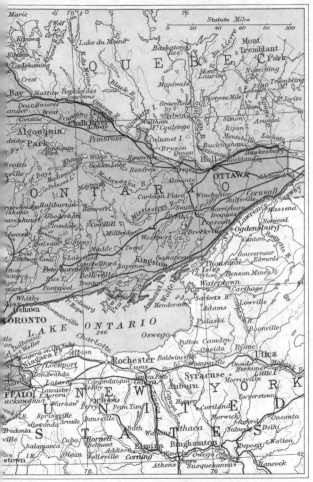

Statute Miles

0   20   40   60   80   100

© — John Bartholomew & Son Ltd. Edinburgh

QUEBEC

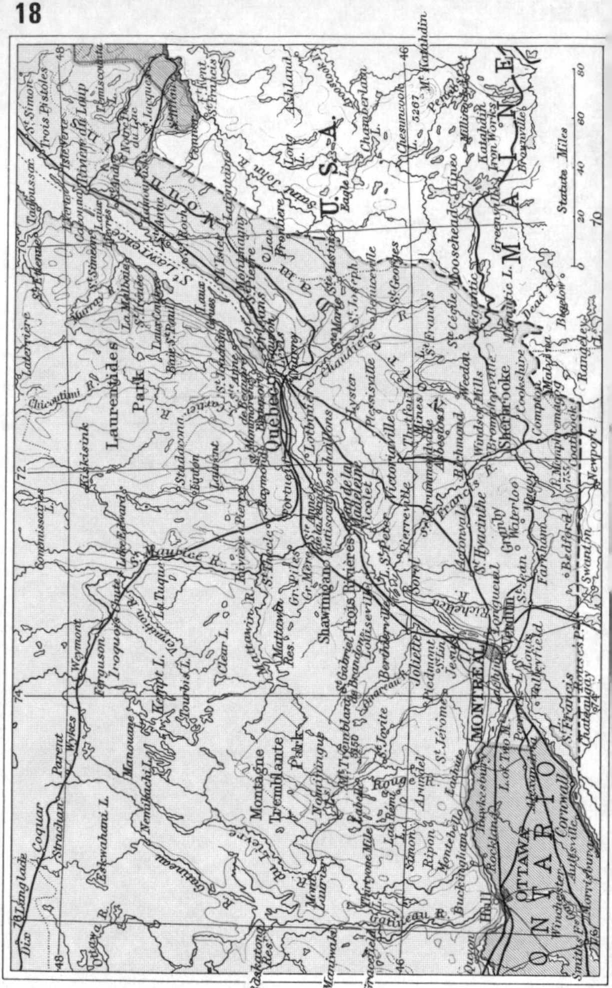

U.S.A.
MAINE
ONTARIO
OTTAWA
MONTREAL
Quebec
Laurentides Park
Sherbrooke
Shawinigan
Maurice R.
St Simon
Trois Pistoles
Chicoutimi R.
Mt. Katahdin
5207

Statute Miles
20 40 60 80

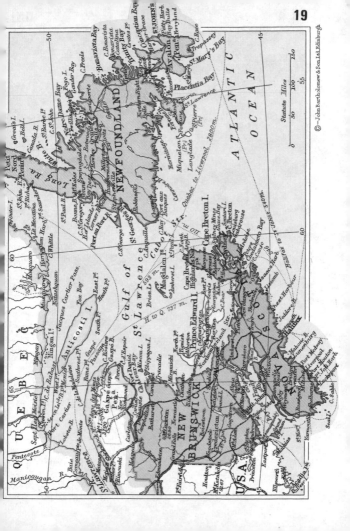

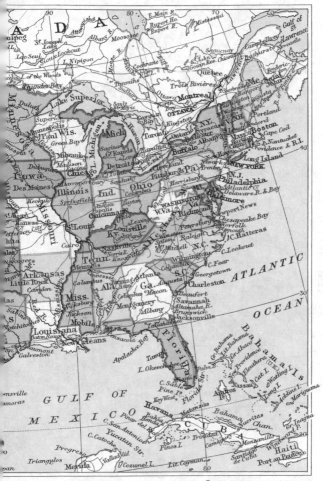

EASTERN STATES

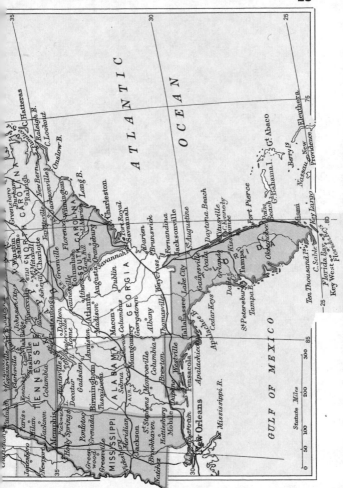

MIDDLE ATLANTIC COAST

24

ERIE AND OHIO BASINS

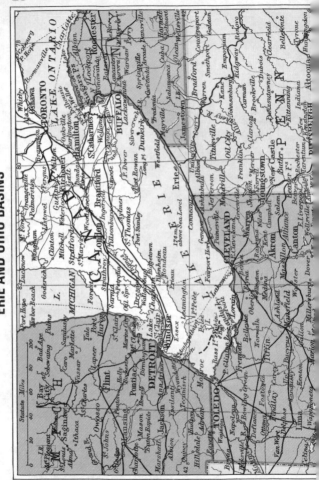

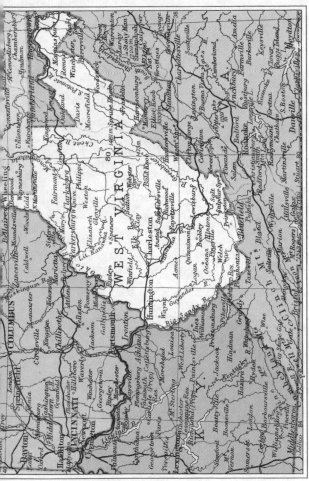

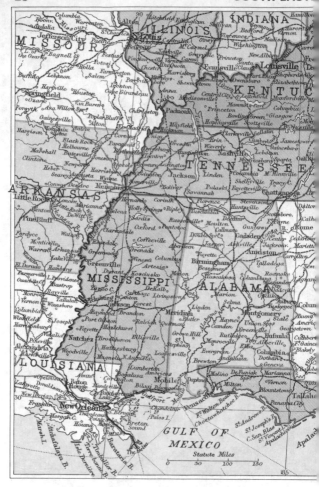

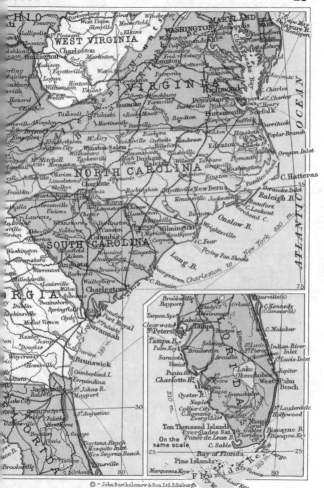

CENTRAL STATES

© – John Bartholomew & Son.Ltd.Edinburgh

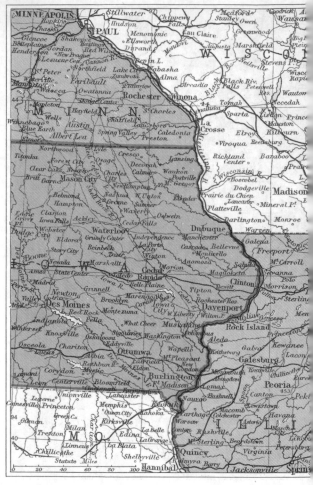

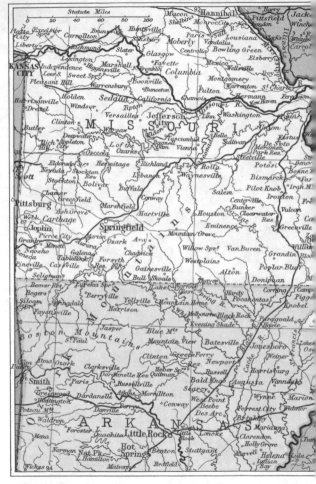

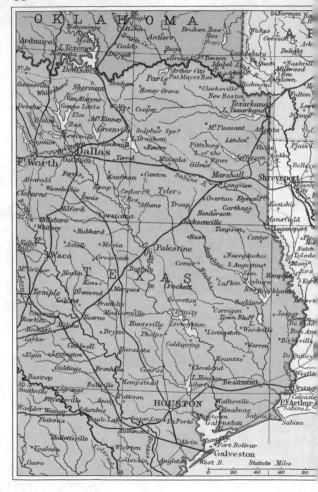

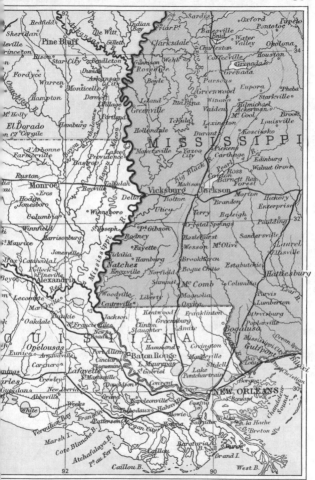

WESTERN STATES

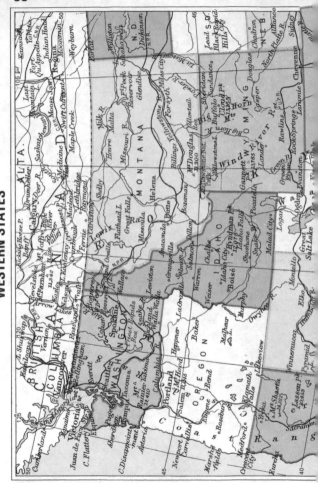

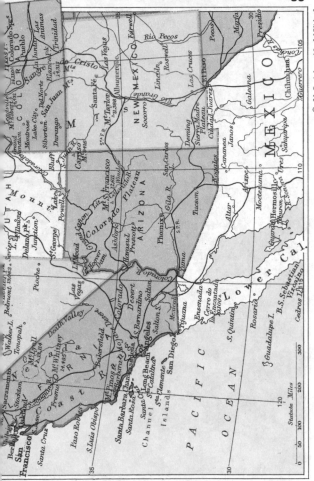

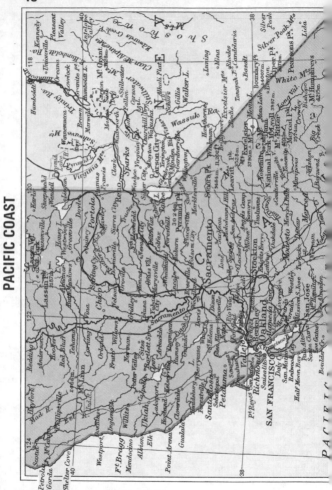

© –John Bartholomew & Son. Ltd Edinburgh.

OCEAN

LOS ANGELES

Long Beach

Santa Barbara Chan.

SANTA BARBARA CHANNEL

Santa Barbara Chan.

SANTA BARBARA ISLANDS

Catalina I.

Santa Cruz I.

St. Rosa I.

San Miguel I.

Bakersfield

Mt Pinos

Tehachapi

Mojave

Mt Whitney

Owens Valley

Lone pine Valley

Trona

Monterey

Pacific Grove

Point Sur

Statute Miles

WASH

Seattle

Victoria

Vancouver

Tacoma

Olympia

Mt Rainier

Portland

C. Flattery

Columbia R.

Statute Miles

0   10   50   100

ALASKA

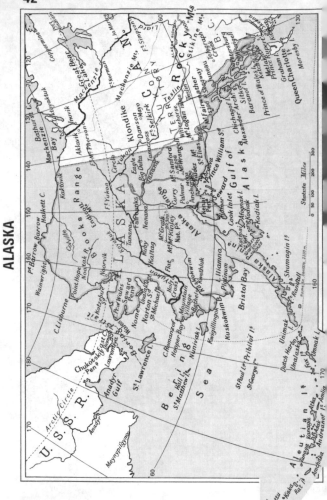

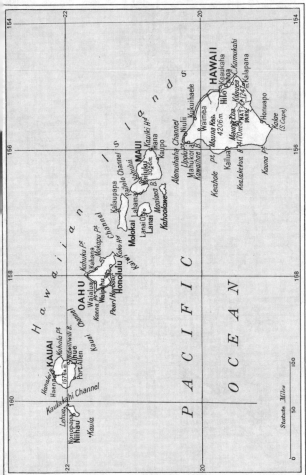

MEXICO AND C. AMERICA

UNITED STATES

ATLANTIC OCEAN

GULF OF MEXICO

PACIFIC OCEAN

CARIBBEAN SEA

CUBA

JAMAICA

BAHAMA IS.

MEXICO

CENTRAL AMERICA

GUATEMALA

HONDURAS

SALVADOR

NICARAGUA

COSTA RICA

Lower California

Sierra Madre

G. of California

Gulf of Darien

Yucatan

Campeche Bay

Tehuantepec

Tropic of Cancer

El Paso, Ciudad Juárez, Chihuahua, Hermosillo, Guaymas, Mazatlan, Culiacan, Durango, Torreon, Zacatecas, Aguascalientes, Guadalajara, Colima, Manzanillo, Morelia, Acapulco, Zacatula, C. Corrientes

Nuevo Laredo, Laredo, Monterrey, Saltillo, Ciudad Victoria, Tampico, Tuxpan, Veracruz, Orizaba, Puebla, MEXICO City, Toluca, Cuernavaca, Oaxaca

Brownsville, Matamoros, Corpus Christi, Galveston, Houston, San Antonio, Austin, Brazos R., Sabine R., Pecos, Rio Grande

New Orleans, Mobile, Pensacola, Tallahassee, Jacksonville, Albany, Savannah, Jackson, Mouths of the Mississippi, Florida Keys, Key West, Florida Strait, Gulf Stream

Progreso, Mérida, Campeche, Yucatan Channel

Habana (Havana), Cienfuegos, Santiago, Windward I., Santo Domingo, Haiti, Kingston, Gr. Cayman

Barranquilla, Cartagena, Bluefields, Managua, San José, Panama

Statute Miles
0 100 200 300 400 500

PACIFIC OCEAN

ATLANTIC OCEAN

WEST INDIES

LESSER ANTILLES

Tropic of Cancer

BAHAMA I. ISLANDS (UK.)

CUBA

GREATER ANTILLES

JAMAICA

HISPANIOLA

Puerto Rico (United States)

HAITI

DOMINICAN REPUBLIC

Santo Domingo

San Juan

CARIBBEAN SEA

Virgin Is.

St. Kitts
Antigua
Guadeloupe (Fr.)
Dominica (UK.)
Martinique (Fr.)
St. Lucia (UK.)
St. Vincent (UK.)
Barbados (UK.)
Grenada (UK.)

TRINIDAD
TOBAGO

SOUTH AMERICA

G. of Venezuela

VENEZUELA

Maracaibo

Barranquilla
Cartagena
Santa Marta

Statute Miles
0 100 200 300

© John Bartholomew & Son Ltd. Edinburgh

SOUTH AMERICA

OCEAN

Equator

CARIBBEAN SEA

CENTRAL AMERICA

Galapagos Is. (Ecu.)

OCEAN

Jamaica
Gr. Cayman
Belmopan
C. Gracias a Dios
Pt. Gallinas
Haiti Dominican Rep. Puerto Rico
Guadeloupe
Barbados
Tobago
TRINIDAD & TOBAGO
Mouths of Orinoco

VENEZUELA
Caracas
Maracaibo
Orinoco
GUYANA
Georgetown
Paramaribo
DUTCH GUIANA
FRENCH GUIANA
Cayenne

COLOMBIA
Bogotá
Quito
ECUADOR
Guayaquil

Galapagos

PERU
Lima
Cuzco

BRAZIL
Brasília
Recife
Salvador (Bahia)
Mato Grosso
R. Amazon
Mouth of Amazon R.
Rio Negro
R. Madeira
R. Roosevelt
R. São Francisco
R. Tocantins
R. Xingu
R. Tapajós
R. Purus
R. Juruá

Selvas
Campos

VENEZUELA, COLOMBIA, GUIANA

Statute Miles

0   100   200   300   400

ATLANTIC OCEAN

CARIBBEAN SEA

St Vincent · Barbados
Grenadines (UK)
· Grenada (UK)

Blanquilla
Margarita
TRINIDAD & TOBAGO
Trinidad

Los Roques
La Guaira
CARACAS
Barcelona
Cumaná
Carúpano

Mouth of the Orinoco

Willemstad
Curaçao (Neth.)
Venezuela G.

Punto Fijo
Coro
Falcón
Valencia
Maracay
Barquisimeto

Pt. Gallinas
Guajira Pen.
Riohacha

Santa Marta
Pte Colombia
Barranquilla
Cartagena

Gulf of Darien
Colón
Panama

C. Marzo

Lake Maracaibo
Maracaibo
Mérida
S. Cristóbal
Cúcuta
Bucaramanga
Pamplona

Medellín
Antioquia
Manizales
Ibagué
Quindío
BOGOTÁ
Tunja
Villavicencio

Buenaventura
Cali
Palmira
Popayán
Pasto

Túquerres
Tulcán
ECUADOR
Cotopaxi

Trujillo
S. Fernando

Barinas
Apure
Puerto Ayacucho
Maipures

Orinoco
Ciudad Bolívar
Caura
Paragua
Caroni
Angostura
El Callao

GUIANA
Georgetown (Demerara)
New Amsterdam
SURINAM
Paramaribo
Roberts
DUTCH
GUIANA

FRENCH GUIANA
Cayenne

Essequibo
Courantyne
Berbice
Kaieteur Falls

Roraima Mts.

Boa Vista

R. Branco
Manaus
Rio Negro
Barcelos

BRAZIL
AMAZONAS

Demini

Japurá
Içá
S. Joaquim
Vaupés
Orinoco
Uaupés
Guainía

COLOMBIA
Meta
Vichada
Guaviare
Caquetá
Cayarí
Yari
Tres Esquinas
Florencia
Caguán

PERU
Iquitos
Amazon
Putumayo
Pebas
Pastaza
Tigre
Curaray

Equator

VENEZUELA

COLOMBIA

Buenaventura
Gorgona Is.
R.Patia
Tumaco
Esmeraldas
Francisco
dernales
QUITO
Manta
ECUADOR
Chimborazo
Riobamba
uayaquil
alinas
Puna
Tumbes
anco
ará
aita
aytu
hura
uja
mbayeque
Chiclayo
Pacasmayo
Trujillo
R.Santa
Chimbote
Casma
Huaraz
Huanuco

Tolima Vol.
Ibague
Girardot
Cali
Popayan
Neiva
Sotara
Tulcan
Moora
Cayambe
Antisana
Cotopaxi
Cuenca
Loja
Barranca
Moyobamba
Chachapoyas
Cajamarca
Pataz
Uchiza
Pucallpa

BOGOTA
Meta
Florencia
Caqueta
Vichada
S.Fernando
de Atabapo
Guaviare
Inirida
Yari
Vaupes
Mitu
Siharu Falls
Japura
Pebas
or
Amazon
Nauta
Leticia
Tabatinga
S.Paulo de
Olivença
Tefes
Jura
R.Tapaia

BRAZIL

Equator
S.Joaquim
Ica
Equator

Iquitos
Maranon
Curaray
Tigre
Pastaza
Napo
Putumaso
Japura

Ucayali
Yavari
(Javari)
Jurua
Acre
Purus
Bermudez
Abuna

Jaen
Huallaga
Ucayali

PERU

pto.Supe
Huacho
LIMA
Callao
Chorillos
Huancavelica
Ayacucho
Chincha
Pisco
Ica

Cerro de Pasco
La
Oroya
Huancayo
CUZCO
Ayaviri
Juliaca
L.Villafro
Acari
Acari R.
Arequipa
Misti
Mollendo
Ilo
Moquegua
Tacna
Arica
Pisagua
Iquique
Rio Loa
Tocopilla
Mejillones

Pto.Maldonado
Trucacamba
Apolobamba
Reyes

Madre de Dios
Riberalta
Madidi
Rio
Branco

Sanhara
Acrim
Mamore

BOLIVIA

Lake
Titicaca
Puno
Ancohuma
Illimani
LAPAZ
Sahama
Oruro
Cochabamba
I.
Poopo
SUCRE
Potosi
Tarapaca
Uyuni
Lagunas
Tupiza
Calama
Atacama
Huanchaca
Quien

CHILE

PACIFIC

OCEAN

Statute Miles
0   100   200   300   400
80   70

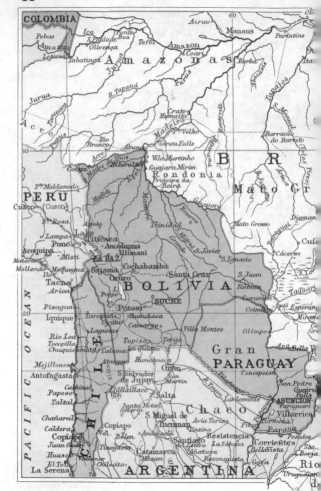

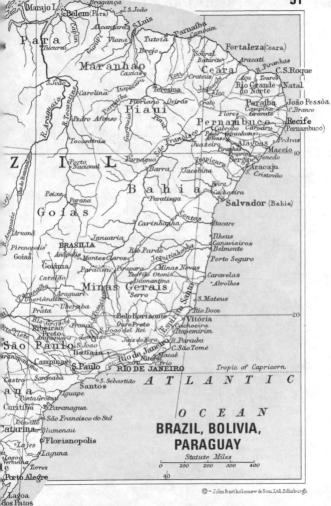

Marajo I.

Bragança

Belem (Para)

el S.João

Alcantara S.Luis

Para

Tucurui

Viana

Tutoia

Parnaiba

Camocim

Fortaleza (Ceara)

Brejo

Sobral Bature

Aracati

Touros

C.S.Roque

Maranhão

Caxias

Crateus

Ceara

Iguatu

Natal

Icó R.Piranhas

Teresina

Jaguaribe

Rio Grande
do Norte

Carolina

Itapecuru

Oeiras

Crato

Paraiba

João Pessôa

Pedro Afonso

Floriano

Piaui

Flores

Campina
Grande

C.Branco

Tocantins

Piraci

Pernambuco

Recife
(Pernambuco)

Parnagua

Juazeiro

Palmares

Alagoas

S.Francisco

Barra

Penedo

Maceió

Paratinga

Jacobina

Japicuru

Sergipe

Aracaju

S. Cristovão

Goias

Bahia

Feira

Cachoeira

Salvador (Bahia)

Carinhanha

Contas

Itacare

Brasilia

Januaria

Ilheus

Andopolis

Rio Pardo

Canavieiros
Belmonte

Goiâna

Jequitinhonha

Porto Seguro

Poraçatu

Prapara

Minas Novas

Caravelas

Catalão

Teofilo Otoni

Diamantina

Abrolhos

Minas Gerais

Serro

Araguari

Uberaba

Belo Horizonte

Rio Doce

Prata

Ouro Preto

Vitória

Franca

S.João del Rei

Cachoeira

Ribeirão

Juiz de Fora

Itapemirim

Preto

R.Paraiba

São Paulo

Itatiaia

S.João

Rio de Janeiro

C.São Tomé

Campinas

S.Paulo

Niteroi

C.Frio

Tropic of Capricorn

Sorocaba

Santos

S.Sebastião

ana

Ponta Grossa

Iguape

Curitiba

Paranagua

A T L A N T I C

Jouville

São Francisco do Sul

O C E A N

Catarina

Blumenau

Lajes

Florianopolis

**BRAZIL, BOLIVIA,
PARAGUAY**

Laguna

Torres

Statute Miles

Porto Alegre

0   100   200   300   400

40

Lagoa
dos Patos

© – John Bartholomew & Son, Ltd. Edinburgh

10

20

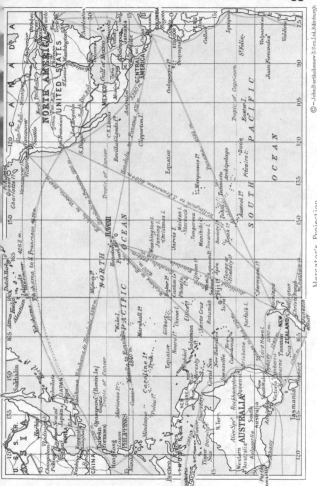

53

© –John Bartholomew & Son, Ltd. Edinburgh

Mercator's Projection

Mercat

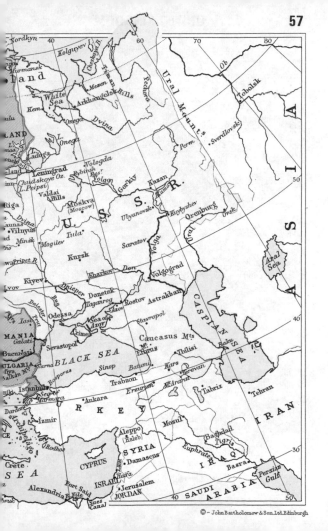

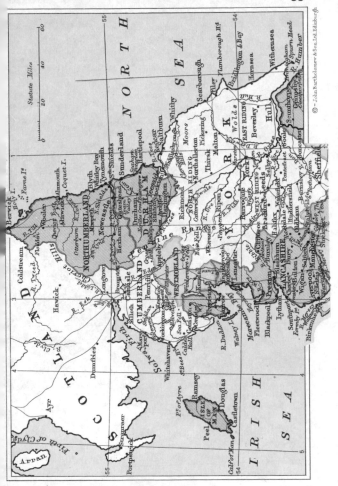

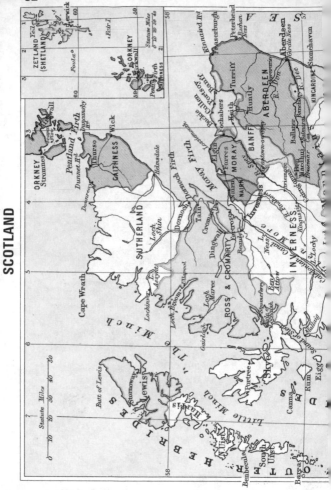

SCOTLAND

IRELAND

SCANDINAVIA

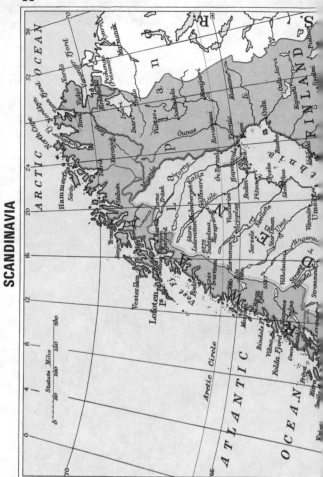

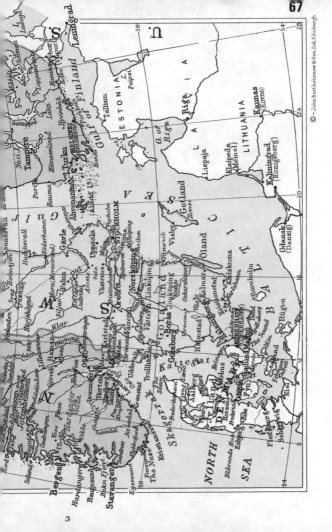

Statute Miles
0 20 40 60 80 100

ATLANTIC

OCEAN

© — John Bartholomew & Son, Ltd. Edinburgh

Statute Miles

NORWAY

SWEDEN

SKAGERRAK

KATTEGAT

JYLLAND

SÆLLAND

FUNEN

LOLLAND

FALSTER

WEST

GERMANY

EAST

HAMBURG

BORNHOLM
(to Denmark)
same scale

© - John Bartholomew & Son, Ltd. Edinburgh.

NETHERLANDS, BELGIUM, LUXEMBOURG

Emden

53

Ems

Rottum

Schiermonnikog

Delfzijl

Bosch

Winschoten

The Dollart

Emmen

GRONINGEN

Groningen

Ameland

Zoutkamp

Assen

Coevorden

Terschelling

FRIESLAND

DRENTE

Harlingen

Leeuwarden

Vliedand

WADDEN

Sneek

ZEE

Meppel

Hoogeveen

OVERIJSSEL

Almelo

Hengelo

Enschede

Texel

Wieringen

IJSSEL

Zwolle

Vecht

Deventer

ZUIDER

Emmeloord

IJssel

Winterswijk

Den Helder

No

ZEE

GELDERLAND

Apeldoorn

HOLLAND

Hoorn

Kampen

Zutphen

Doesburg

Alkmaar

Enkhuizen

Harderwijk

Zijpe

Beverwijk

Lelystad

Ede

Arnhem

Zaandam

Amersfoort

IJmuiden

Bussum

Zeist

Rhin

Aalten

Haarlem

AMSTERDAM

Nijkerk

Katwijk aan Zee

Leiden

UTRECHT

Tiel

Nijmegen

Waal

Scheveningen

Utrecht

Maas

's GRAVENHAGE

Zoudelft

(HOLLAND)

Vaart

Rijn

's Hertogenbosch

(THE HAGUE)

Gouda

Lek

Hook van Holland

Vlaardingen

Rotterdam

Gorinchem

Grave

Harlingvliet

Oudewater

Dordrecht

Goeree

Oude

Waal

Rosendaal

Schouwen

Oost S.

Zierikzee

Walch

N O R T H

52

S E A

3

4

5

6

7

32

Statute Miles

10 20 30 40 50

0 10 20 30 40

53

52

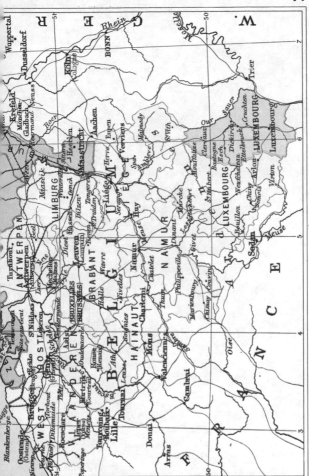

SWITZERLAND

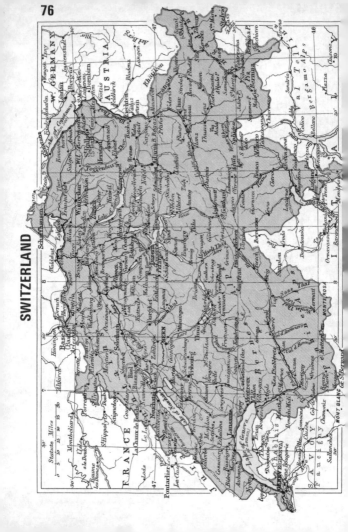

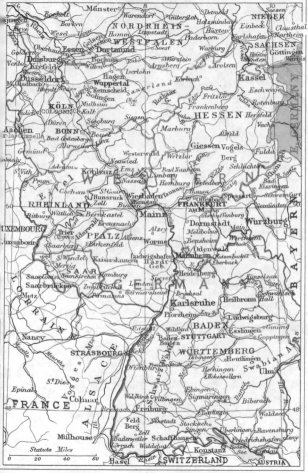

© - John Bartholomew & Son.Ltd.Edinburgh.

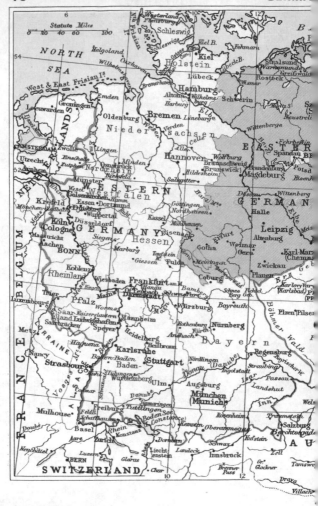

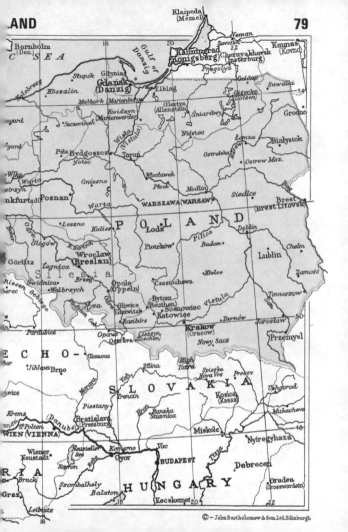

Statute Miles
0   50   100   150

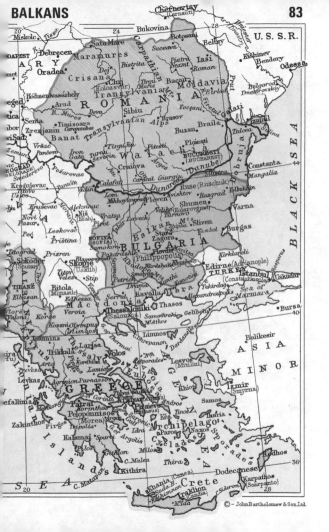

NORTH ITALY

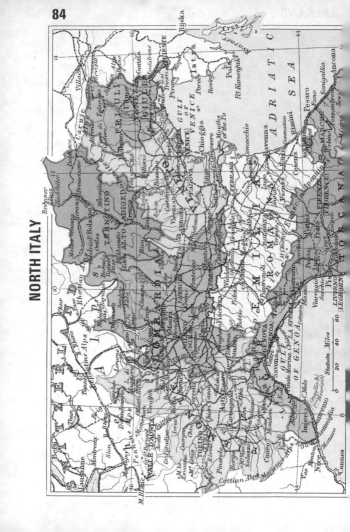

WESTERN U.S.S.R.

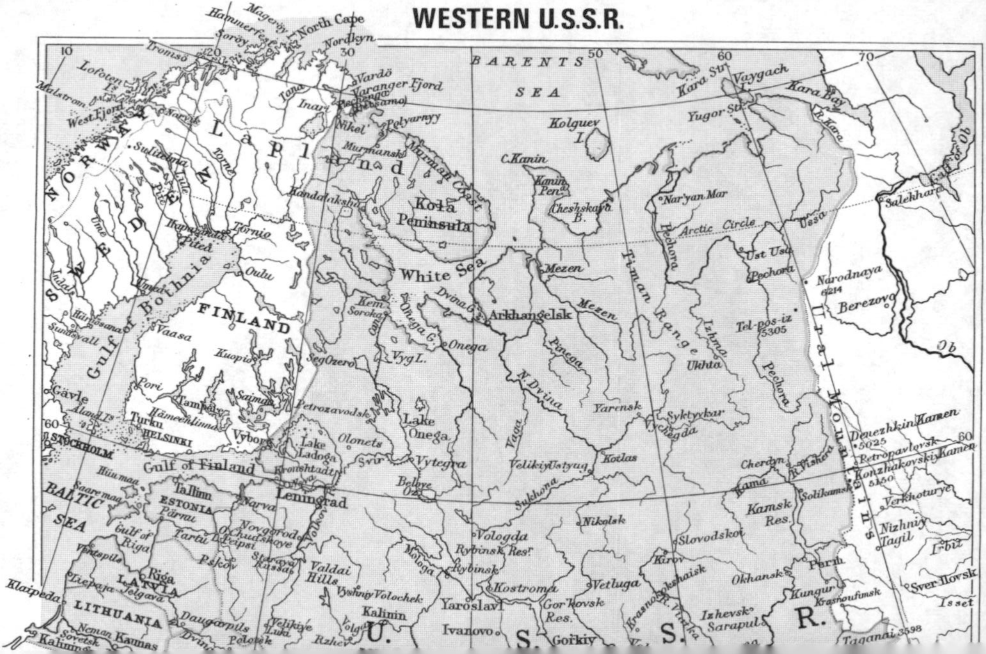

BARENTS SEA

Ural Mountains

Arctic Circle

Timan Range

Kola Peninsula

White Sea

Onega G.

Lake Onega

Lake Ladoga

FINLAND

Gulf of Finland

Gulf of Bothnia

BALTIC SEA

NORWAY

SWEDEN

ESTONIA

LATVIA

LITHUANIA

Leningrad

Helsinki

Stockholm

Murmansk

Archangelsk

Pechora

N. Dvina

Ob

Tel-pos-iz 5305

U. S. S. R.

GORKY

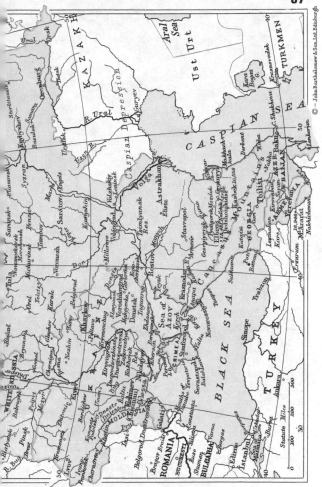

UKRAINE

CASPIAN SEA

BLACK SEA

TURKEY

CAUCASUS

GEORGIA

ARMENIA

AZERBAIJAN

BAKU

Mouths of the Volga

Derbent

Makhachkala

Buinaksk

GROZNY

Ordzhonikidze

Elbrus

TBILISI

Kutaisi

Batum

Sukhumi

Poti

Sochi

Novorossiysk

Krasnodar

Stavropol

Kizlyar

Mt. Ararat

Kars

Artvik

Trabzon

Erzurum

R. Araxes

R. Aras

Nakhichevan

Stepanakert

Shusha

Kirovabad

Sevan

Yerevan

Leninakan

Echmiadzin

Akhalkalaki

Akhaltsikhe

Borzhomi

Gori

Telavi

Nukha

Mirbechaur

Shemakha

Agdam

Kuba

Sheki

Statute Miles
0   50   100   150

SOVIET CENTRAL ASIA

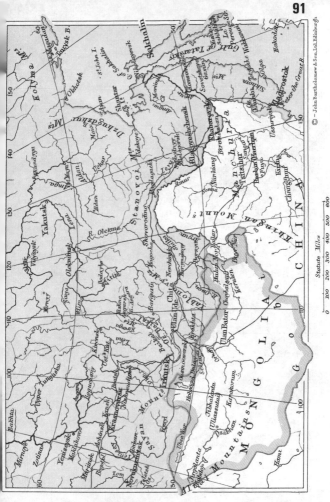

© – John Bartholomew & Son.Ltd.,Edinburgh

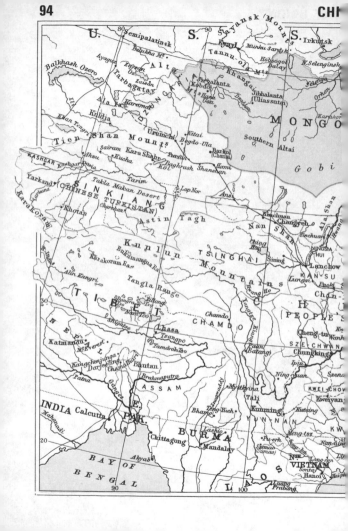

JAPAN

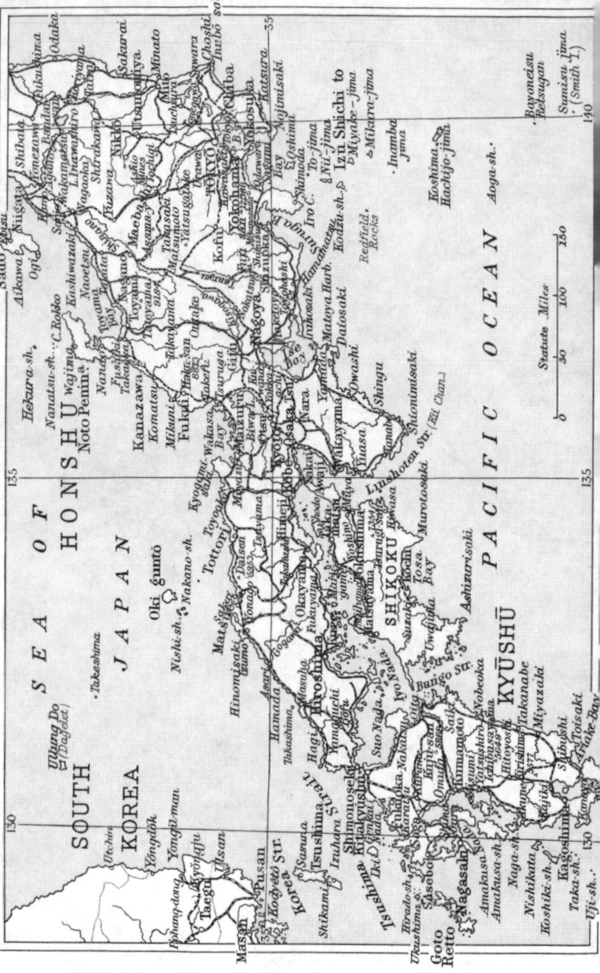
SEA OF JAPAN
HONSHU
SHIKOKU
KYŪSHŪ
PACIFIC OCEAN
SOUTH KOREA
Tokyo
Yokohama
Nagoya
Kyoto
Osaka
Kobe
Hiroshima
Nagasaki
Kagoshima
Niigata
Kanazawa
Fukui
Toyama
Nagano
Shizuoka
Okayama
Himeji
Wakayama
Matsuyama
Kochi
Fukuoka
Shimonoseki
Kumamoto
Miyazaki
Oita
Pusan
Taegu
Masan
Tsushima
Goto Retto
Sado
Oki gunto
Izu Shichi to
Statute Miles
0 50 100 150

© - John Bartholomew & Son.Ltd. Edinburgh

© – John Bartholomew & Son, Ltd. Edinburgh

© — John Bartholomew & Son, Ltd. Edinburgh

Palk Strait
Kankesanturai
Karaitivu
P.t Pedro
Velanai I.
Kts. Jaffna
Kachchcheri
Delft I.
Elephant Pass
Chunnakan
Iraniham
Kilinochchi
Palk Bay
NORTHERN
PROVINCE
Mullaittivu
Rameswaram
Dhanushkodi
Talaimannar
Adam's Bridge
Mannar
Murankan
Pooneryn
Palampiddi
Kokkilai
Marichchukkaddi
Vavuniya
Nilaveli
Trincomalee (Tiru Kona Malai)
Foul P.t
Karativo I.
NORTH CENTRAL
Anuradhapura
Mihintale
Palampiddan
Mitur
Kalpitiya
PROVINCE
Kala Oya
Katiraveli
Puttalam
NORTH
Kekirawa Habarane
Sigiriya
Welikanda
Vendelus Bay
Palukuddah
Valaichchenai
WESTERN
Dambulla
Polonnaruwa
Nikaweratiya
Maho
PROVINCE
Nalanda
Chenkaladi
Batticaloa
Chilaw
Wariyapola
Kurunegala
Matale
CENTRAL
EASTERN
PROVINCE
Amparai
Kalmunai
Polgahawela
PROVINCE
Kandy
Peradeniya
Senanayake Samudra
Negombo
Kegalla
Gampola
Bibile
Gal Oya
COLOMBO
Gampaha
Nawalapitiya
Pidurutalagala
8281
Ragala
Nawara Eliya
Badulla
UVA
Mt Lavinia
WESTERN
Talawakele
Adams Pk.
Totapella
7353
7165
Bandarawela
PROVINCE
Pottuvil
Moratuwa
Panadure
PROV.
Ramapura
Bakingoda
Wellaway
Kalutara
SABARAGAMUWA
Balangoda
Opanake
Telulla
Okanda
Beruwala
Matugama
Moragalla
Rakwana
Buyes
Little Basses
Bentota
Great Basses
Ambalangoda
SOUTHERN PROVINCE
Hakmana
Galle
Gintota
Tangalla
Hambantota
Matara
(Matruha)
Dondra H.d
Weligama

INDIAN OCEAN

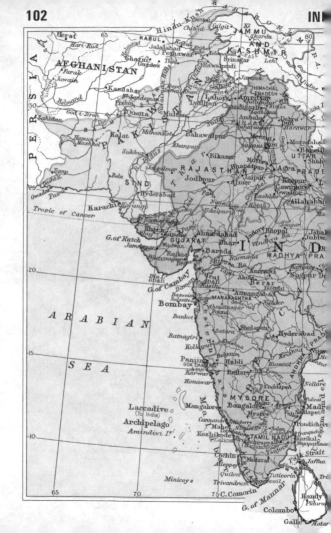

Statute Miles
0   100   200   300   400   500

T a n g l a M t s.
Di-chu
B E T.   C H I N A
Zilling Tso
Dangra   Nag Chu
Yum
Tengri Nor
Lhasa   30

Brahmaputra or Tsangpo
Mt.Everest
Kinchinjunga
Chumalhari
THIMPHU
BHUTAN   Sadiya
NEPAL   Taipuelisa   Tibrugarh Pitao
Gangtok   Brahma...   K A C H I N S
Darjeeling   Jorhat   Myitkyina
Gauhati   Nowgong   Teng-yueh   Tali
MEGHALAYA   Silchar   Mogaung   Kunming
EAST   Imphal   Bhamo   25
IHAR PAKISTAN MANIPUR   Katha
Dacca   TRIPURA
Kalewa   Mogok   Kunlong Lashio
Murshidabad   Chittagong   Yeu   Percy
Burdwan   Sagaing Mandalay   Kiang Lao-kai Song bo
WENSA   Chandpur   Ava Amarapura   Kiang Hung
Calcutta   Myingyan   Kuanglung M'Sing
Kurseong   Chaira   Maktila   Chiang
R.Hooghly   Mouths of Ganges   Rai   Luang
SSA   Cuttack   Nau   Prabang
ESWAR   Akyab   Minbu   20
Puri   Chilka L.   Karenni Chiang Mai
Ganjam   Prome   Lampun   THAILAND
Sandoway   Pegu   (SIAM)
hapatnam   Rangoon
Bassein   Martaban
C.Negrais   Moulmein
Amherst   15
Praparis   G. of Martaban
B A Y   O F   Tavoy   KRUNG THEP (BANGKOK)
Prakan
Andaman   Mergui
Islands   Mergui   Tenasserim
(To India) Port Blair Archipelago   Gulf of
B E N G A L   Kra Isthmus   Siam   10
Victoria Pt.
Phangnga
Songkla
85   90   Nicobar Is. 95   100

© — John Bartholomew & Son.Ltd.Edinburgh

UTTAR PRADESH

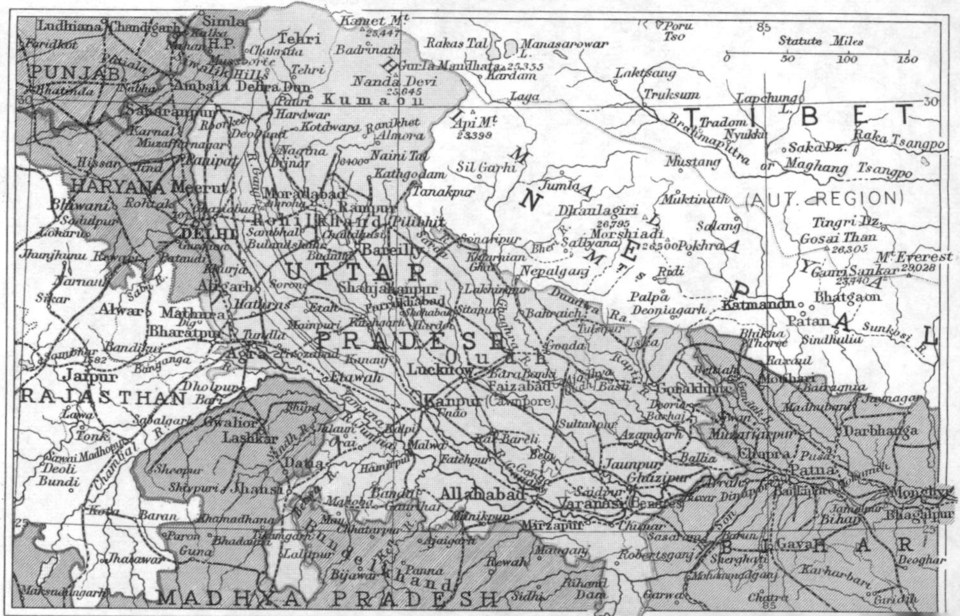

Statute Miles
0   50   100   150

T I B E T
(AUT. REGION)

Manasarowar
Rakas Tal
Raka Tsangpo
or Maghang Tsangpo

Kamet Mt. 25,447
Badrinath
Kailas Parbat 22,028
Mt. Everest 29,028
Gosai Than 26,305

H.P.
Simla
Chandigarh
Ludhiana

PUNJAB

HARYANA

DELHI

RAJASTHAN

U T T A R   P R A D E S H

M A D H Y A   P R A D E S H

B I H A R

Lucknow
Kanpur
Allahabad
Agra
Gwalior

Nanda Devi
25,645

Naini Tal

Kumaon

N E P A L

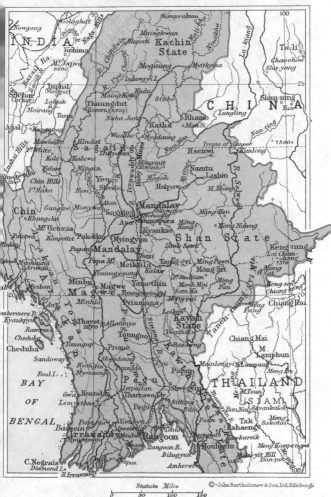

Statute Miles
0   50   100   150

© John Bartholomew & Son Ltd. Edinburgh

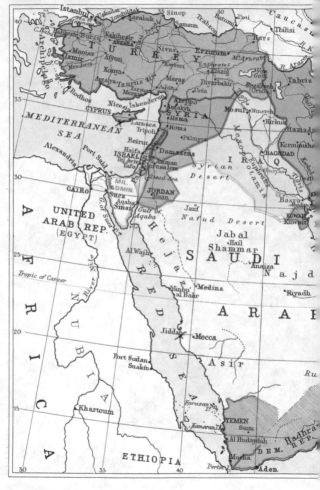

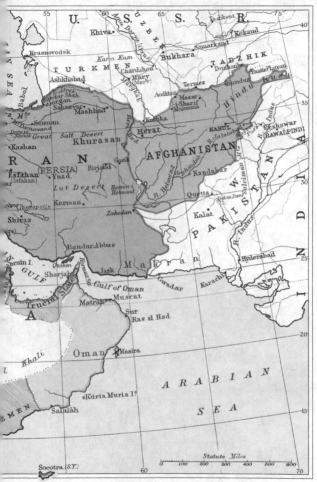

U. S. S. R.

55 60 65 75 40

Khiva

Krasnovodsk

Karakum (Oxus)

Tashkent
Kokand

Samarkand

Bukhara

TURKMEN

Chardzhou

TADZHIK

Dushanbe

Ashkhabad

Mary
(Merv)

Termez

Kunduz

Bain Plateau

Bandar-Shah
Gorgan
Sabzevar
Mashhad

Andkhui

Mazar-i-Sharif
Maimana

HINDU KUSH

Kushka

Meshed

Herat

KABUL

Peshawar
RAWALPINDI

Semnan
Mt Damavand

Salt Desert

KHURASAN

Jalalabad

I R A N
(PERSIA)

Birjand

AFGHANISTAN

Esfahan
(Isfahan)
Yazd

Ghazni

Kashan

Lut Desert

Hamun-i-Helmand

Kandahar

Kerman

Zahedan

Quetta

Bolan Pass

P A K I S T A N

Kalat

Shiraz

35

30

25

Persepolis

Bandar Abbas

Qeshm

Hormuz Str.

Jask

M A K R A N

Sharjah

GULF

Trucial States

Muscat

Gwadar

Karachi

Hyderabad

Matrah

Sur
Ras al Had

I N D I A

Khali

Oman

Masira

20

A R A B I A N

YEMEN

Salalah

Kuria Muria Is.

S E A

15

Socotra (S.Y.)

60 70

Statute Miles
0 100 200 300 400 500 600

© – John Bartholomew & Son, Ltd, Edinburgh

TURKEY

ISRAEL, LEBANON

Statute Miles
0   20   40   60

MEDITERRANEAN SEA

Tel Kalakh
En Nahr el Kebir
Homs
Homs
Bahret
El Mina
Tripoli
(Tarabulus)
Ehden
Hermil
ElKaa
Batrun
Bsherri
Lebya
RasBaalbek
Sadad
El Qaryatein
En
Nebk
Junie
Zahle
Baalbek
BEIRUT
el Hadeth
LEBANON
Riyaq
Jerud
Quteife
Qasr Zigal
Sidon
(Saida)
Nabatiye
Rasheiya
Zebdani
Es Salihiye
Dumeir
to Port Said I.P.C. 120mi. 230 m.
Nel-Qasimiye
Hasbaya
Qatana
DAMASCUS
(DAMAS)
Tyre
(Sur)
Qiryat
Shemona
Mt Hermon
Banyas
Kiswe
SYRIA
Bint Jubail
El Hule
Quneitra
Mesmiye
Nahariyya
Acre
(Akko)
Es Sanamein
El Leja
W.el Rarts
B.of Acre
Safad
(Zefat)
L. of Tiberias
Nawa
Eho
Haifa
Atlit
Shefaram
Tiberias
Sheikh Miskin
Es Suweidiya
Jebel ed
Nemara
Druz
Zikhron Yaaqov
Nazareth
Afula
Mazera
Deras
Busra
JEBEL ED DRUZ
Salkhad
Caesarea
Hadera
Beyt Shean
Irbid
Imtan
ISRAEL
Jenin
Ajlun
Mafraq
Tulkarm
Nablus
Jarash
H-50 Pipe Line
Tel-Aviv
Yafo
Petah Tiqva
ISRAEL MIL.
ADMIN.
Salt
Zarqa
Ramla
Lydda (Lod)
Suweileh
AMMAN
Qasr el Azraq
Rehovot
Jericho
Naur
El Mawaqqar
W.Rajil
Ashdod
JERUSALEM
EL QUDS ESH SHERIF
Jiza
Qalat
ed Daba
El Hazim
Ashqelon
Rest
Bethlehem
Madaba
Gaza
Hebron
(El Khalil)
Dhiban
Khan Yunis
Arad
Khan ez Zabib
Rafah
Karak
JORDAN
Beersheba
Sdom
El Qatrana
Dimona
Tarin
Yeroham
ISRAEL MIL.
ADMIN.
Subeita
Et Tafila
Qal'at el Hasa
NEGEV
Juf ed
Darawish
Bayir
El Qusaima
Shaubak
Ain Kadeis
Qal'at Uneiza

PETRA

© –John Bartholomew & Son Ltd. Edinburgh.

AFRICA

EUROPE

ASIA

ATLANTIC OCEAN

Caspian Sea

Black Sea

MEDITERRANEAN SEA

RED SEA

SAUDI ARABIA

Paris
Lisbon
Strait of Gibraltar
Madeira I. (Port.)
Canary Is. (Sp.)
Teneriffe
Cape Verde I.

MOROCCO
ALGERIA
TUNISIA
Tunis
Tripoli
LIBYA
Fezzan
Murzuq
Ghat

SAHARA
SPANISH SAHARA
MAURITANIA
SENEGAL
Dakar
Bathurst
Bissau
PORT. GUINEA
GUINEA

MALI
Timbuktu
NIGER
Zinder
Sokoto
UPPER VOLTA
N. NIGERIA
Kaduna
IVORY
DAHOMEY

CHAD
L. Chad
Tibesti
Zouar

UNITED ARAB REP. (EGYPT)
Nile
Aswan
Libyan Desert
Port Said
Suez
Alexandria
Damietta

Istanbul
Ankara
Cyprus
Jerusalem

SUDAN
Khartoum
Wadi Halfa
Port Sudan

ERITREA
Addis Ababa
Djibouti
Berbera
Socotra I.
Cape Guardafui

Casablanca
Essaouira

Mecca
Medina

U.A.R. (EGYPT), LIBYA

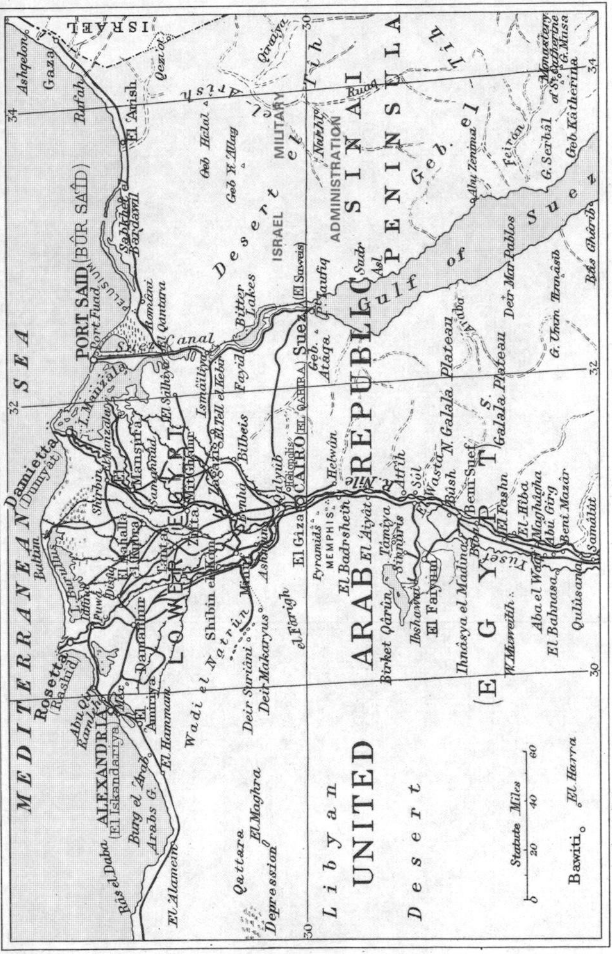
MEDITERRANEAN SEA
ISRAEL
Ashqelon
Gaza
Rafah
El Arish
Qezi'ot
Qiraiya
PORT SAID (BÛR SA'ÎD)
Port Fuad
Sabkhet el Bardawil
Români
El Qantara
Suez Canal
Ismâ'iliya
Bitter Lakes
Fayid
Suez (El Suweis)
Pt. Taufiq
Geb. Atâqa
Damietta (Dumyât)
L. Manzala
Rosetta (Rashîd)
ALEXANDRIA (El Iskandariya)
Abu Qir
L. Burullus
Baltîm
Tanta
Zagazig
Bilbeis
Benha
Qalyub
Heliopolis
CAIRO (EL QÂHIRA)
El Gîza
Pyramids
MEMPHIS
Helwân
El Badrsheîn
El 'Aiyât
Atfîh
El Faiyûm
Birket Qârûn
Beni Suef
El Wâsta
Bûsh
El Fashn
Maghâgha
Beni Mazâr
Samâlût
El Bahnasa
Qulûsana
Ihnâsya el Madina
LOWER EGYPT
Wadi el Natrûn
Deir Suriâni
Deir Makaryus
El Farigh
El Maghra
Qattara Depression
El Alamein
Râs el Daba
Burg el 'Arab
El Hammam
Arabs G.
Libyan Desert
UNITED ARAB REPUBLIC
(EGYPT)
Desert
Bawiti
El Harra
N. Galala Plateau
S. Galala Plateau
Deir Mar Pablos
G. Umm Tenâsib
Râs Ghârib
Gulf of Suez
Abu Zenima
Feirân
G. Serbâl
Geb. Kâtherîna
Monastery of St. Catherine
G. Mûsa
SINAI PENINSULA
Geb. el Tîh
Nakhl
ISRAEL MILITARY ADMINISTRATION
Geb. Helal
Geb. Y. 'Allag
Ruag
Statute Miles
0 20 40 60
30
32
34

NORTH-WEST AFRICA

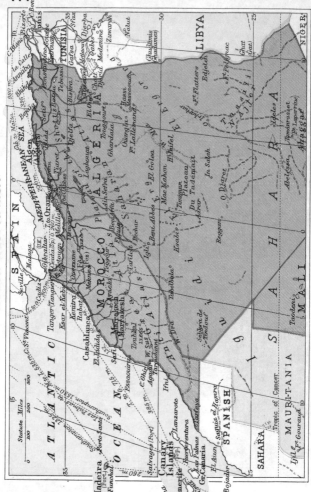

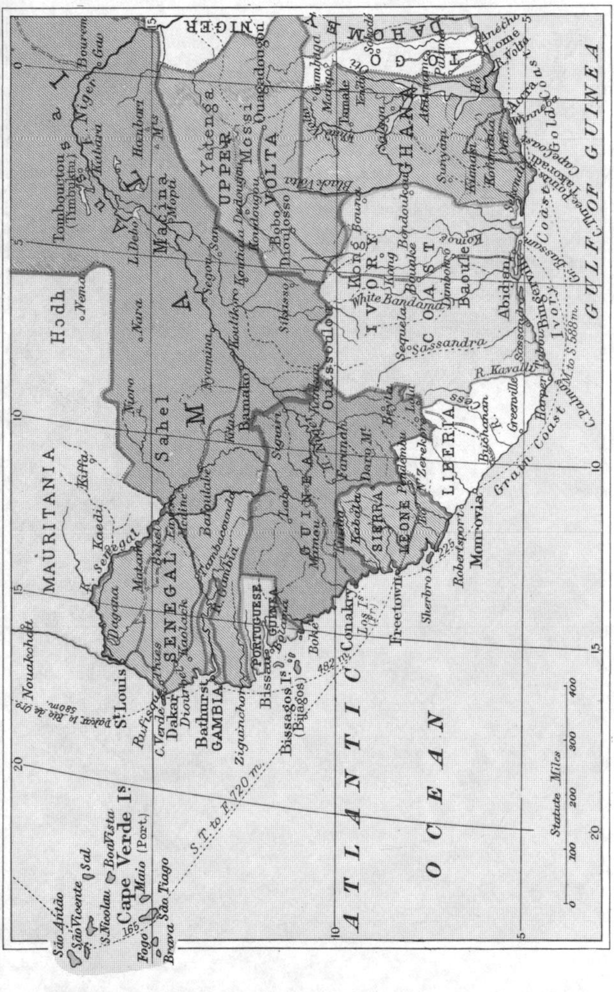
MAURITANIA
Hodh
Sahel
M A L I
Tombouctou (Timbuktu)
NIGER
UPPER VOLTA
Ouagadougou
DAHOMEY
TOGO
GHANA
SENEGAL
GAMBIA
PORTUGUESE GUINEA
GUINEA
SIERRA LEONE
LIBERIA
IVORY COAST
Cape Verde Is (Port.)
St Louis
Dakar
Bathurst
Bissau
Conakry
Freetown
Monrovia
Abidjan
Accra
Bamako
Lomé
Grain Coast
Ivory Coast
Gold Coast
ATLANTIC OCEAN
GULF OF GUINEA
Statute Miles
0 100 200 300 400

© John Bartholomew & Son Ltd. Edinburgh

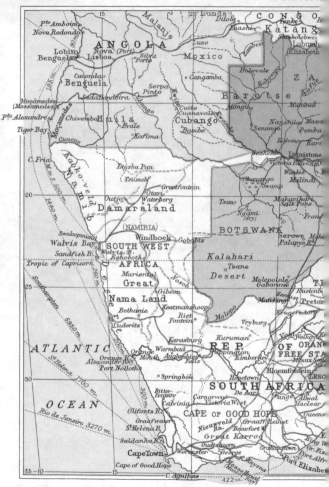

Njombe

TANZANIA

Kasama
Kaponda
Livingstonia
L. Bangweulu
Songea
Masasi
Mtwara
C.Delgado
Gāe
Comoro I.
Moheli
Anjouan

Chitambo
Chisteche
Mzimba
Vila
Cabral
Legenda
Rovuma
Ibo
P.to Amelia
Comoro Is.
Mayotte

Chipawa
Kota Kota
Ft Jameson
Salima
Domira B.
Arroio
Lurio
Lurio B.
Memba

Zumbo
Francungo
Zomba
L. Chilwa
Nampula
Tumbe
Mecunta
Moçambique
Moçambique

Tete
Ft Darwin
Blantyre
Chiromo
Manje
Mokuba
Nacala

Kildonan
Shamya
Chemba
Salisbury
Mashona Land
Sena
Quelimane
390m.

Rusape
V.a Monica
Umtali
Ft Melsetter
Chinde
Zambezi

bele La
Fort Victoria
Zimbabwe
Beira
Nova Sofala

Nicholson
Bazaruto I.
Bassas
da India

Beitbridge
Limpopo
Gaza

Kruger
Nat
Park
Inhambane
C. Corrientes

Chibut

Vila de João Belo
Lourenço Marques
Delagoa Bay

Swazi
L.d
Piet Retief
Zulu
Land
Sta Lucia Bay

NATAL
Pietermaritzburg
Durban
Scottsburgh
Shepstone

St Johns

INDIAN

OCEAN

MOÇAMBIQUE

MOÇAMBIQUE CHANNEL

St André
Soalala
MALAGASY REP.
Maintirano

C.d'Ambre
Diego Suarez
Nossi Bé
Vohémar
Narendry B.
Analalava
Antalaha
Majunga
Mananara
Antongil B.
G.St
André
Soalala
Maevatanana
I. Ste Marie
Maintirano
Alaotra L.
Androva
Tamatave
Tananarive
(Antananarivo)
Andevoranto
Ankaratra Mts
Antsirabe
Makanoro

Morondava
MALAGASY REP.
(MADAGASCAR)
Mananjary
INDIAN

Ambohibe
Mangoky
Fianarantsoa
Manakara
OCEAN

Tuléar
Farafangana
Betroka
Vangaindrano
Tropic of Capricorn

Ft Dauphin

C. Ste Marie

On the same scale

Statute Miles
0   100   200   300

© - John Bartholomew & Son Ltd. Edinburgh

SARAWAK

BORNEO
Samarinda

Manado
Ternate
Halmahera
Is.

MOLUCCAS

Manokwari
Biak
Japen
Pt d'Urville

Makassar Str.
G. of Tomini
Sula Is.

CELÉBES

Butung

Bandjarmasin
Laut
Makasar

Buru
Ambon
Seram

Kaji I.

IRIAN BARAT

NEW

INDONESIA

Banda Sea

Aru Is.
Kolepom

Java Sea
Madura
Flores Sea

Tanimbar Is.

Arafura Sea

JAVA
Bali
Lombok
Solor Is.
Wetar
Alor
Dili

Weasel I.

Torr
Thurs

Sumbawa
Sumba
Flores
Roti
Kupang

Timor

Melville
Bathurst I.
Darwin
Rum Jungle
Melville I.

Melville B.
Cohourg Pen.

Gulf of
Carpentar

Timor Sea

Cambridge G.
Queens land
Arnhem Land
Katherine

Groote Eylandt

Collier B.
Wyndham

Victoria R.
Birdum

Barkly
Burketown
Pellheland

King Sd.
Black Rocks
Derby
Fitzroy R.

Weldale Is.

L. Leveque
Broome

NORTHERN

Tennant
Creek
Mount Isa

Great Sandy
Desert
Mt. Wilson
Central Mt. Stuart

TERRITORY

Port Hedland
Roebourne

L. Mackay

Macdonnell Ra.

Exmouth G.
Onslow
N. West Cape

Mt. Bruce
Ashburton R.

L. Macdonald
Gibson
Disappointment
Desert

L. Hopkins
L. Amadeus

Alice Springs

AUSTRAL

Shark B.
Carnarvon

Murchison R.
Meekatharra
Wiluna

Steep Pt.

L. Austin

WESTERN

Great Victoria Desert

SOUTH AUSTRALIA

Ooldatta

L. Torre

Geraldton

AUSTRALIA

Kalgoorlie
Nullarbor
Northam Coolgardie Boulder
Perth L. Lefroy
Fremantle York R.
Geographe B.
C. Naturaliste
Bunbury

Plain
Eucla
L. Cowan

Maralinga
L. Gairdner

Ipteron
Port Pir

Augusta
Whyalla

Great
Australian Bight

Spencer G.
St. Vincent G.

Bl

King George Sd.
C. Leeuwin
Albany

Esperance
Recherche
Archip.

Kangaroo I.
Encounter B

Warrnam

INDIAN OCEAN

TA

Statute Miles

0   500   1000

Equator

Gilbert (UK) Is

Admiralty Is
Manus
New Hanover
Bismarck
Archipelago
Madang
NEW
GUINEA
G. of Papua
Moresby
York
Rabaul
Kokopo
New Britain
New Ireland

Bougainville
Choiseul
Solomon
Islands
Isabel
New Georgia
Guadalcanal
Malaita
San Cristobal

Samarai
China Str.
Louisiade Arch.
Rennell

Sta Cruz Is (UK)
Ndeni

CORAL SEA

Willis I.

Espiritu Santo
Banks Is.

Malekula
New
Hebrides
(UK & Fr.)
Efate

Chesterfield Is. (Fr.)

P A C I F I C

Fiji (UK) Is

Eromanga

Halifax B.
Townsville
Port Denison
Mackay

Rockhampton

New
Caledonia
(Fr.) Noumea

Loyalty Is

Tropic of Capricorn

O C E A N

Great Barrier Reef

Hervey B.
Fraser or
Sandy I.
Moreton Bay
Brisbane
C. Byron
Grafton

Bundaberg
Maryborough

SLAND
A

Norfolk I.
(Aust.)

Port Macquarie

Lord Howe I.
(Aust.)

OUTH WALES
Maitland
Newcastle
Wollongong
Sydney
Canberra
Bathurst
Goulburn

Kermadec
Is (NZ)

Kosciusko

RIA
Melbourne

Cape Howe
Wilsons Prom.

T A S M A N

North C.

Bass Strait
Furneaux Is.
Launceston

S E A

Auckland
East C.

obart

NEW
ZEALAND

New Plymouth
Hamilton
Cook Str.
Nelson
South I.
Hokitika

Gisborne
Napier
Wellington

North I.

Christchurch
Chatham
Is

West C.

Dunedin

Stewart I.

150   160   180   40

© — John Bartholomew & Son,Ltd.Edinburgh

Statute Miles
0   100   200

C · John Bartholomew & Son.Ltd.Edinburgh

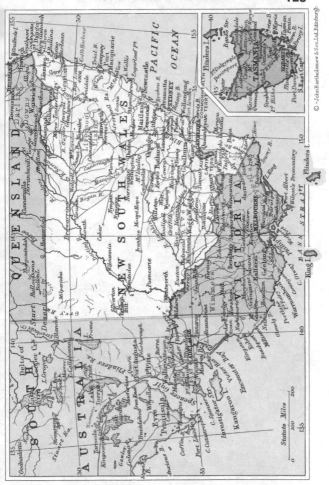

© John Bartholomew & Son. Ltd. Edinburgh

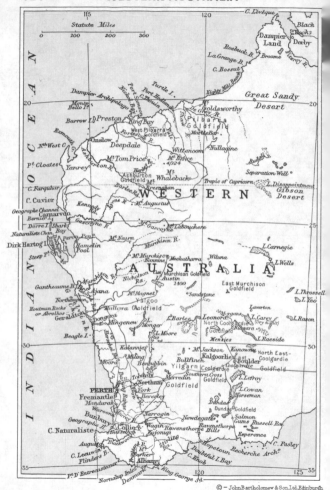

© — John Bartholomew & Son Ltd. Edinburgh.

AUSTRALIA

NEW GUINEA

PAPUA

Bismarck Archipo.

New Britain

Solomon Is.

CORAL SEA

ARAFURA SEA

Arnhem Land

Gulf of Carpentaria

New Caledonia (French)

New Hebrides

FIJI Is.

Viti Levu

Vanua Levu

WESTERN SAMOA

Tonga or Friendly Is.

Tokelau or Union Is.

Phoenix Is.

Ellice Is. (U.K.)

Gilbert Is. (U.K.)

Marshall Islands

Caroline Islands (Trust Territory U.S.)

Palau

PACIFIC OCEAN

Equator

Tropic of Capricorn

Statute Miles

© John Bartholomew & Son Ltd, Edinburgh

Statute Miles

Divisions coloured
are statistical areas

Statute Miles

0   50   100

Divisions coloured
are statistical areas

© –John Bartholomew & Son,Ltd.,Edinburgh

Capetown
C. of Good Hope
C. Agulhas

Gough I.

Antarctic Circle

Marion I.
Prince Edward I.

Bouvet I.

Average Limit of Drift Ice

S. Georgia Dep.
S. Orkney Is.
S. Sandwich Is.

Scotia Sea

Falkland Is.

S. Shetland Is.
Elephant I.

British Antarctic Territory

Dronning Maud Land

C. Norvegia

Enderby Ld.
Kemp Ld.
Mac Robertson Ld.

Weddell Sea

Coats
Land

Caird Ct.

Filchner

Prince
Harald Ld.

Cape Horn

Falkland Is.

Drake Passage

Graham Land

Palmer Pen.

Biscoe Is.

Charcot I.

Alexander I.

Antarctic
Pen.

Princess
Elizabeth Ld.

Wilhelm II Ld.

Queen Mary Ld.

A N T A R C T I C A

Bellingshausen
Sea

Peter I. I.

Ellsworth
Highland

Hillary 3rd Jan 1958
Amundsen
1911

SOUTH
POLE

Fuchs 19 Jan 1958

Scott
1912

Knox Coast

Sabrina Coast

Amundsen
Sea

Marie Byrd
Land

Roosevelt I.

Scott
1902-3

Budd Land

Banzare Coast

Antarctic
Circle

Fuchs Ice

King
Edward VII Ld.

Little
America

Ross
Sea

Ross Dependency

Mt. Erebus
Franklin I.
Lady Newnes B.
Coulman I.
Possession I.
C. Adare

Balleny Is.

Victoria
Land

South
Magnetic
Pole

Terre Adélie

King George V Ld.

Oates Ld.

Campbell I.

Macquarie I.

Tasmania
Hobart

Antipodes I.
Bounty I.
50° S.

Auckland
Is.

C. Howe

Dunedin
Stewart I.

South I.

Tasman
Sea

Sydney

Christchurch
Wellington
North I.

NEW ZEALAND

Cook Str.

Auckland

ANTARCTICA

Statute Miles
0   500   1000

© — John Bartholomew & Son, Ltd. Edinburgh

Gazetteer

Aberdeen, city and port, N.E. Scotland
Abidjan, port and cap. of Ivory Coast, Africa
Accra, cap. of Ghana, West Africa
Aconcagua, highest peak of Andes; 23,035 ft.
Acre, state, Brazil
Addis Ababa, cap. of Ethiopia
Adelaide, cap. of South Australia
Afghanistan, an independent state on the N.W. frontier
    of Pakistan; cap. Kabul
Ahmedabad, town and cap. of Gujarat, India
Akron, city, Ohio, S. of Cleveland
Al Bayda', town, Libya
Alabama, state, U.S.A.; cap. Montgomery
Alagoas, state, Brazil
Alaska, state of U.S.A., in N.W. America
Albania, rep., on the Balkan Peninsula; cap. Tiranë
Albany, city and cap. of New York
Alberta, prov., Canada; cap. Edmonton
Albuquerque, town, New Mexico
Alexandria, city and port, U.A.R.
Algeria, rep., on north coast of Africa
Algiers (Alger), cap. of Algeria
Allentown, city, Pennsylvania, N.W. of Philadelphia
Alma Ata, town, Kazak, N.E. of Frunze
Amapá, state, Brazil
Amarillo, town, Texas
Amazonas, state, Brazil
Amazon, river, S. America, 4,000 m. long

American Samoa, prov., Pacific Ocean
Amman, cap. of Jordan
Amsterdam, cap. and port, Netherlands
Amur, river, U.S.S.R., enters Sea of Okhotsk
Anaheim, town, California
Andhra Pradesh, state, India
Andorra, republic, Pyrenees Mts.
Andros Island, Bahamas, W. Indies
Angola, Portuguese col., W. Africa; cap. Luanda
Anguilla, island, Leeward Is., W. Indies
Anhwei, prov., China
Ankara, cap. of Turkey, S.E. of Istanbul
Annapurna, mt. Nepal, 26,504 ft.
Antigua I., Leeward Is., W. Indies
Ararat, Mount, Turkey, 16,946 ft.
Argentina, rep., S. America; cap. Buenos Aires
Arizona, state, W. U.S.A.; cap. Phœnix
Arkansas, state, S. U.S.A.; cap. Little Rock
Armenia, rep., U.S.S.R.; cap. Yerevan
Ascension Island, S. Atlantic Ocean
Assam, state, India; cap. Shillong
Asuncion, port and cap. of Paraguay
Athens (Athínai), city and cap. of Greece
Atlanta, cap. of Georgia, U.S.A.
Auckland, prov. and city, North I., N.Z.
Austin, cap. of Texas, on Colorado River
Australia, state, cap. Canberra, smallest continent
Austria, rep., Cent. Europe; cap. Vienna
Azerbaijan, rep., U.S.S.R.; cap. Baku
Badrinath, mt., India/Tibet; 23,190 ft.
Baghdad, city and cap. of Iraq
Bahama Islands, Brit., group, W. Indies
Bahia, state, Brazil

Bahrain, island and state, Persian Gulf
Baikal, Lake, U.S.S.R.; area 13,500 sq. m.
Baku, port and cap. of Azerbaijan
Balearic Isles, group, in Mediterranean
Balkhash, Lake, Kazak, U.S.S.R.
Baltimore, city and port, Maryland
Bamako, cap. of Mali, on R. Niger
Bandar Seri Begawan, town and cap. of Brunei
Bandarpunch, mt., India
Bangalore, town and cap. of Mysore, India
Bangkok (Krung Thep), city and cap. of Siam
Bangui, town, cap. of Cent. Afr. Rep.
Barbados, island, W. Indies
Barbuda, island, Leeward Is., W. Indies
Barcelona, city and port, Spain
Basildon, new town, Essex, England
Bata, town and cap. of Equat. Guinea
Bathurst, cap. of Gambia, W. Africa
Baton Rouge, city, cap. of Louisiana
Bear Lake, Great, N.-W. Terr., Canada
Beaumont, town, Texas, S.E. of Dallas
Beirût, city and cap. of Lebanon
Belfast, port and cap. of N. Ireland
Belgium, kingdom, W. Europe; cap. Brussels
Belgrade, Beograd
Belmopan, cap. of Br. Honduras
Belo Horizonte, city, Brazil, N. of Rio de Janeiro
Benghazi, port, Libya, N. Africa
Benoni, town, S. Africa
Beograd (Belgrade), city, cap. of Yugoslavia
Berkeley, city, California, on San Francisco B.
Berlin, city, Germany, on R. Spree
Bermuda, island group, N. Atlantic

Berne (Bern), cap. of Switzerland
Bhutan, state, in the Himalayas
Bihar, state, India; cap. Patna
Birkenhead, port, Cheshire, England
Birmingham, city, Alabama
Birmingham, city, Warwicks, England
Blackburn, town, Lancs, England
Blackpool, seaside town, Lancs, England
Bloemfontein, cap. of O.F.S., S. Africa
Bogotá, cap. of Colombia, S. America
Bolivia, rep., S. America; cap. Sucre
Bolton, town, Lancs, England
Bombay, city and port, W. India, cap. of Maharashtra
Bonn, city and cap. of W. Germany
Bordeaux, city and port, S.W. France
Boston, city and port, cap. of Mass., U.S.A.
Botswana, rep., S. Africa, cap. Gaborone
Bournemouth, town, Hants, England
Bradford, city, Yorks, England
Brahmaputra, river, Asia, flows into Bay of Bengal,
    1800 m. long
Brasília, federal capital of Brazil
Brazil, rep., S. America; cap. Brasília
Brazzaville, town, cap. of People's Rep. of the Congo,
    Central Africa
Bremen, town, W. Germany
Bridgetown, cap. of Barbados
Bridgeport, city, Long Island Sd., Conn.
Brighton, seaside tn., E. Sussex, England
Brisbane, port and cap. of Queensland
Bristol, city and port, Glos. and Som., Eng.
British Columbia, prov., W. Canada
British Honduras, col., Cent. Amer., cap. Belmopan

British Solomon Is., group, Pacific Oc.
Brunei, state, N.W. Borneo
Brussels (Bruxelles), cap. of Belgium
Bucuresti (Bucharest), city, cap. of Romania
Budapest, city and cap. of Hungary
Buenos Aires, fed. cap. of Argentina
Buffalo, city, New York, on Lake Erie
Bujumbura, town, cap. of Burundi
Bulawayo, town, S: Rhodesia
Bulgaria, rep., Balkan Pen.; cap. Sofia
Burma, rep., E. of India; cap. Rangoon
Burundi, rep., central Africa
Byelorussia, rep., U.S.S.R., cap. Minsk.
Caicos Islands, W. Indies, N. of Hispaniola
Cairo, cap. of U.A.R., on the Nile
Calcutta, city, port and cap. of W. Bengal
Calgary, city, Alberta, S. of Edmonton
California, state, W. U.S.A.; cap. Sacramento
Cambodia, Khmer Republic
Cambridge, co. town, Cambs., England
Cambridge, city, Mass., suburb of Boston
Camden, city, New Jersey, on Delaware River
Cameroun, republic, Central Africa, cap. Yaoundé
Canada, state, N. America, cap. Ottawa
Canary Islands, Span. group, off N.W. Africa
Canberra, fed. cap. of Australia
Canton, town, Ohio
Cape of Good Hope (Cape Province), prov. of
     Republic of South Africa
Cape Town, port and cap. of Cape Prov.
Cape Verde Islands, group, Atlantic Oc., off N.W. Africa
Caracas, cap. of Venezuela
Cardiff, city and cap. of Wales

Casablanca, port and naval base, Morocco
Cayenne, port and cap. of French Guiana
Cayman Islands, group, W. Indies
Ceará, state, N.E. Brazil
Central African Rep., cap. Bangui
Ceuta, port and naval base, Morocco
Ceylon, rep., I. off S. India ; cap. Colombo
Chad, rep., Africa ; cap. Fort Lamy
Chad, Lake, Africa
Channel Islands, off N.W. coast of France
Charles Louis, Mt., New Guinea
Charlotte, city, N. Carolina, S.W. of Raleigh
Chattanooga, tn., Tennessee, on Tennessee R.
Chekiang, prov., China
Chelyabinsk, prov. and town, U.S.S.R.
Chengtu, city, Szechwan, China
Chicago, city, Illinois, on L. Michigan
Chile, rep., S. America ; cap. Santiago
Chimborazo, peak in the Andes, Ecuador
China, rep., cap. Peking
Chinghai, prov., China
Christchurch, city, S. Island, New Zealand
Christmas Island, Polynesia, Pacific Ocean
Chumalhari, mt., Bhutan ; 23,996 ft.
Chungking, port, Szechwan, China, on Yangtse Kiang
Cincinnati, city, Ohio, on Ohio River
Citlaltepetl, mt., Mexico, 17,879 ft.
Cleveland, city, Ohio, on L. Erie
Cocos Is., group, Pacific Ocean
Cologne (Köln), city, W. Germany, on Rhine
Colombia, rep., S. America ; cap. Bogotá
Colombo, port and cap. of Ceylon
Colorado, state, W.-cent. U.S.A. ; cap. Denver

Columbus, cap. of Ohio, U.S.A.
Columbus, town, Georgia
Comoro Islands, Mozambique Channel
Conakry, port and cap. of Guinea, W. Africa
Congo, river, central Africa, flows 3000 m. to Atlantic Oc.
Congo, Dem. Rep. of, Africa; cap. Kinshasa
Congo, People's Rep. of, W. Africa; cap. Brazzaville.
Connecticut, state, N.E. U.S.A.; cap. Hartford
Cook Islands, Polynesia, Pacific Ocean
Cook, Mt., N.Z.
Copenhagen (København), cap. of Denmark
Cork, city and co., Rep. of Ireland
Corpus Christi, town, Texas
Costa Rica, republic, Central America, cap. San José
Cotapaxi, mt., Ecuador; 19,344 ft.
Coventry, city, Warwicks, England
Cuba, island and rep., West Indies, cap. Havana
Cyprus, island and rep., E. Mediterranean, cap. Nicosia
Czechoslovakia, rep., central Europe, cap. Prague
Dacca, city, E. Bengal, cap. of E. Pakistan
Dahomey, rep., W. Africa; cap. Porto Novo
Dakar, port and cap., Senegal, West Africa
Dallas, city, Texas, E. of Forth Worth
Damascus, city and cap. of Syria
Damavand, mt., Iran, 18,934 ft.
Danube, river of Cent. Europe, length 1740 m.
Dar es Salaam, port, and cap., Tanzania
Dayton, city, Ohio, W.S.W. of Columbus
Dearborn, town, Michigan
Delaware, river, rises in New York and flows to
    Delaware B.
Delaware, Atlantic state, U.S.A.; cap. Dover
Delhi, city and cap. of India

Denmark, kingdom, Europe; cap. Copenhagen
Denver, cap. of Colorado, U.S.A.
Derby, co. town, Derbyshire, England
Descabezado, mt., Chile
Des Moines, city and cap. of Iowa
Detroit, city and port, Michigan
Dikh-tau, mt., U.S.S.R.
Djakarta, tn. and port, Java; cap. of Indonesia
Dnepropetrovsk, town, Ukraine, S.W. of Kharkov
Dominica, island, Leeward Is., W. Indies
Dominican Rep. (Santo Domingo), Hispaniola West
    Indies, cap. Santo Domingo
Donetsk, town, Ukraine, S.E. of Kharkov
Dortmund, town, W. Germany, N.E. of Cologne
Dresden, tn., E. Germany, E.S.E. of Leipzig
Dublin, city, port, county and cap. of Rep. of Ireland
Dudley, town, Worcester, England
Duluth, city and lake port, Minnesota
Dundee, cy. & pt., Angus, Scot., on R. Tay
Dunedin, town, South I., New Zealand
Durban, port, Natal, on Indian Ocean
Düsseldorf, tn., W. Germany, on the Rhine
East London, port, Cape Province
Ecuador, rep., S. America
Edinburgh, cap. of Scotland, on Firth of Forth
Edmonton, cap. of Alberta, Canada
Elbrus, highest peak, Caucasus, U.S.S.R.
Elizabeth, city, New Jersey, W. of Brooklyn
Ellice Islands, British group in the Pacific, N. of Fiji
El Paso, town, Texas, on Rio Grande
El Salvador, rep., Cent. Amer., cap. San Salvador
England, kingdom, with Wales forms the S. portion of
    Great Britain

Equatorial Guinea, state, W. Africa

Erie, Lake, between Ontario and U.S.A.

Erie, town, Pennsylvania

Espírito Santo, state, Brazil

Essen, town, W. Germany

Estonia, rep., U.S.S.R.; cap. Tallinn

Ethiopia (Abyssinia), kingdom, E. Africa, cap. Addis Ababa

Etna, Mount, volcano, Sicily, 10,741 feet

Euphrates, river, W. Asia, flows 1700 m. to the Persian Gulf

Evansville, town, Indiana, on Ohio river

Everest, mt. peak, Himalayas, highest in the world, 29,028 ft.

F.T.A.I.=French Territory of the Afars and the Issas

Faeroes, The, Dan. islands in N. Atlantic Oc.

Falkland Islands Dependency, Brit. col., S. Atlantic

Fernando de Noronha, state, Brazil

Fernando Póo, isl., Equat. Guinea, W. Africa

Fès, town, Morocco, E. of Rabat

Fiji Islands, state, in Pacific Ocean

Finland, republic, Europe; cap. Helsinki

Finsteraarhorn, Switzerland, Bernese Alps

Flint, town, Michigan

Florida, a S. Atlantic state, U.S.A.; cap. Tallahassee

Fort Lamy, tn. and cap. of Chad, Africa

Fort Wayne, city, Indiana, S.E. of Chicago

Fort Worth, city, Texas, W. of Dallas

France, republic, W. Europe; cap. Paris

Frankfurt-am-Main, city, W. Germany

Freetown, cap. of Sierra Leone, Africa

French Guiana, prov., S. America

French Terr. of the Afars and the Issas (F.T.A.I.); cap. Djibouti

Fresno, town, California
Fuji-san, mt., Japan, S.W. of Tokio, 12,388 ft.
Fukien, province, China
Gaborone, cap. of Botswana
Gabon, rep., Cent. Africa; cap. Libreville
Gambia, river and rep., W. Africa; cap. Bathurst
Ganga, river, India, flows 1,500 miles into B. of Bengal
Ganges= Ganga
Gangtok, town and cap. of Sikkim
Gary, town, Indiana
Gateshead, town, Durham, opp. Newcastle upon Tyne
Geelong, city, Victoria, S. of Bendigo
Genova, city and port, N.W. Italy, on G. of Genoa
Georgetown, cap. of Guyana
Georgia, S. Atlantic state, U.S.A.; cap. Atlanta
Georgia, republic, U.S.S.R.; cap. Tbilisi
Germany, E., rep., Europe
Germany, W., rep., Europe
Germiston, town, S. Africa
Ghana, rep., W. Africa; cap. Accra
Gibraltar, Br. fortress and town, S. Spain
Gilbert Islands, British group, Pacific Ocean
Glasgow, city and port, Scotland, on the Clyde
Glendale, town, California
Goiás, state, Brazil
Gorkiy (Nizhni Novgorod), city, U.S.S.R., E. of Moscow
Göteborg, port, Sweden, on Gota river
Grand Rapids, city, Michigan, N.W. of Detroit
Grays Thurrock, town, Essex, England
Great Salt Lake, Utah, U.S.A.
Greece, kingdom, S.E. Europe; cap. Athens
Greenland, Danish island, N. America
Greensboro, town, N. Carolina

Grenada, island, W. Indies, Windward Is.
Guadalajara, city, Mexico
Guadeloupe, island, Leeward Is., W. Indies
Guam, island, Marianas Is., Pacific Ocean
Guanabara, state, Brazil
Guatemala, rep., central America
Guatemala City, cap. of Guatemala
Guinea, rep., W. Africa; cap. Conakry
Gujarat, state, W. India; cap. Ahmedabad
Guyana, rep., S. America; cap. Georgetown
Hague, The ('s-Gravenhage), cy., seat of govt.,
  Netherlands
Haiti, rep., Hispaniola, W. Indies; cap. Port-au-Prince
Halifax, port and cap. of Nova Scotia
Hamburg, city and port, W. Germany, on Elbe
Hamilton, city, Ontario, S.W. of Toronto
Hammond, town, Indiana
Hanoi, cy. and cap. of N. Vietnam
Hannover, town, W. Germany
Harbin, town, N.E. China, on Sungari river
Hartford, town, Connecticut
Haryana, state, N. India
Havana, port and cap. of Cuba, W. Indies
Hawaii, largest of the Hawaiian Islands and state,
  U.S.A.; cap. Honolulu
Heilungkiang, prov., China
Helsinki, port and cap. of Finland
Himachal Pradesh, state, N. India
Hobart, city and cap. of Tasmania
Honan, prov., Central China
Honduras, Brit., col., Cent. America; cap. Belmopan
Hong Kong, British Island and col., S. China
Honolulu, cap. of Hawaii, on Oahu Is.

Hopei, prov., China
Houston, town and port, Texas, U.S.A.
Huddersfield, town, Yorks., England
Hull, port, Yorks., England, on the Humber
Hunan, prov., China
Hungary, rep., Cent. Europe; cap. Budapest
Hupeh, prov., China
Huron, Lake, bet. Canada and United States
Hwang Ho, river, China, enters G. of Pohai
Hyderabad, town, Andhra Pradesh, India
Iceland, rep., N.W. Europe; cap. Reykjavik
Idaho, W. state of U.S.A.; cap. Boise
Illampu, mt., Bolivia; 21,490 ft.
Illimani, mt., Bolivia; 22,579 ft.
Illinois, N. cent. state, U.S.A.; cap. Springfield
India, rep., S. Asia; cap. Delhi
Indiana, N. central state of U.S.A.
Indianapolis, city and cap. of Indiana
Indonesia, rep., E. Indies; cap. Djakarta
Indus, river, Pakistan, flows to Arabian Sea
Inner Mongolia, aut. reg., China
Iowa, N. cent. state, U.S.A.; cap. Des Moines
Ipswich, co. town of Suffolk, England
Iran (Persia), kingdom, W. Asia; cap. Tehran
Iraq, rep., Asia; cap. Baghdad
Ireland, island, W. of Great Britain, comprising Rep. of
    Ireland and N. Ireland
Islamabad, fed. cap. of Pakistan, N. of Rawalpindi
Israel, rep., S.W. Asia
Istanbul (Constantinople), town, Turkey
Italy, rep., S. Europe; cap. Rome
Ivory Coast, republic, W. Africa; cap. Abidjan
Jackson, town and cap. of Mississippi

Jacksonville, city, Florida, N.E. of Tampa
Jamaica, island, West Indies; cap. Kingston
Jammu & Kashmir, state, India
Jan Mayen, island, Arctic Ocean
Japan, state, E. Asia
Jersey City, town, New Jersey, on Hudson R.
Jerusalem (El Quds esh Sherif), city, Israel-Jordan
Johannesburg, largest city of Transvaal, S. Africa
Jordan, kingdom and river, W. Asia; cap. Amman
Juncal, mt., S. America; 20,367 ft.
Jungfrau, mt., Bernese Alps, Switzerland
K2, mt., Kashmir, W. Himalayas; 28,250 ft.
Kabul, cap. of Afghanistan on Kabul river
Kamet, mt., Uttar Pradesh; 25,447 ft.
Kampala, town and cap. of Uganda, N.E. of Entebbe
Kangchenjunga, mt., Himalayas; 28,146 ft.
Kanpur, city, Uttar Pradesh, India
Kansas, S. central state of U.S.A.; cap. Topeka
Kansas City, town, Missouri, on Missouri river
Kansas City, town, Kansas, E.N.E. of Topeka
Kansu, prov., China
Karachi, town and port, West Pakistan
Kathmandu, cap. of Nepal, E.N.E. of Lucknow
Kazakhstan, republic, central U.S.S.R.
Kazan, town, U.S.S.R., N.E. of Stalingrad
Kazbek, mt., U.S.S.R.
Kentucky, an E central state, U.S.A.; cap. Frankfort
Kenya, rep., E. Africa; cap. Nairobi
Kenya, Mt., Africa
Kerala, state, S. India; cap. Trivandrum
Khan Tengri, mt., China; 23,620 ft.
Kharkov, city, Ukraine, S. of Moscow
Khartoum, cap. of Sudan

Khmer Republic, state, S.E. Asia, cap. Phnom-Penh
Kiangsi, prov., China
Kiangsu, prov., China
Kiev (Kiyev), city, cap. of Ukraine
Kigali, town and cap. of Rwanda
Kilimanjaro, mt., Tanzania; 19,340 ft.
Kingston, port, naval base and cap. of Jamaica, W. Indies
Kinshasa, cap. of Dem. Rep. of Congo
Kirgizia, rep., U.S.S.R.; cap. Frunze
Kirin, prov., China
Kitakyushu, city, Kyushu, Japan
Kitchener, town, Ontario, W. of Toronto
Knoxville, city and river port, Tennessee
Kobe, town, Honshu I., Japan
Korea, N. and S., reps., E. Asia
Kota Kinabalu, town and cap. of Sabah, E. Malaysia
Kraków (Cracow), city, Poland, on R. Vistula
Krasnoyarsk, town, U.S.S.R., E. of Tomsk
Krivoi Rog, town, Ukraine, N.E. of Odessa
Kuala Lumpur, tn., Selangor, cap. of W. Malaysia
Kuching, town and cap. of Sarawak, E. Malaysia
Kuwait, state on Persian Gulf
Kuwait City, cap. of Kuwait
Kuybyshev (Samara), tn., on Volga, U.S.S.R.
Kwangchow (Canton), city and port, S.E. China
Kwangsi-Chuang, aut. reg., China
Kwangtung, prov., China
Kweichow, prov., China
Kyoto, city, Honshu I., Japan, N.E. of Osaka
Ladoga, Lake, U.S.S.R., on border of Finland
Lagos, port, cap. of Nigeria, S. of Ibadan
Lahore, cap. of W. Pakistan, on Ravi River
Lansing, cap. of Michigan, U.S.A.

Laos, kingdom, S.E. Asia; cap. Vientiane
La Paz, city and dep., Bolivia, S. America
La Plata, river, Argentina
Latvia, rep., U.S.S.R.; cap. Riga
Lebanon, state, W. Asia; cap. Beirut
Leeds, city, Yorks, England
Leeward Islands, Lesser Antilles, W. Indies
Leicester, co. town of Leicestershire, England
Leipzig, city, E. Germany, S.S.W. of Berlin
Lena, river, U.S.S.R., flows to Arctic Ocean; 2,850 m. long
Leningrad, city, U.S.S.R., near Lake Ladoga
Lesotho (Basutoland), state, S. Africa
Liaoning, prov., China
Liberia, rep., West Africa; cap. Monrovia
Libreville, tn. and cap. of Gabon, Cent. Africa
Libya, rep., N. Africa; caps. Tripoli and Benghazi
Liechtenstein, princ., E. Switz.; cap. Vaduz
Lille, town, France, S.E. of Calais
Lima, city and cap. of Peru
Lincoln, town, cap. of Nebraska
Lisbon (Lisboa), city, naval base and cap. of Portugal, on River Tagus
Lithuania, rep., U.S.S.R.; chief town Vilnius
Little Rock, cap. of Arkansas, U.S.A.
Liverpool, city and port, Lancs, England
Llullaillaco, mt., Chile; 22,057 ft.
Lódz, town, Poland, S.W. of Warsaw
Logan, Mount, Yukon, N.W. Canada; 19,850 ft.
Lomé, cap. of Togo, W. Africa
London, cap. of England and U.K., on the Thames
London, port of entry, Ontario, S.W. of Toronto
Londonderry, co. and town, N. Ireland

Long Beach, town, California, U.S.A.
Los Angeles, city, California, S.E. of San Francisco
Louisiana, state, U.S.A.; cap. Baton Rouge
Louisville, city, Kentucky, on the Ohio River
Lourenço Marques, town and cap. of Mozambique
Lower Hutt, town, N. Island, N.Z.
Luanda, port and cap. of Angola, W. Africa
Lubbock, town, Texas
Lusaka, cap. of Zambia, central Africa
Lü-ta, port, Kwangtung, China
Luton, town, Beds., England
Luxembourg, grand Duchy and town, W. Europe
L'vov, town, Ukraine
Lyons, city, France, S.E. of Paris
Macao, island (Portuguese), S. China
Mackenzie, river, N.W. Terr., Canada
McKinley, Mount, Alaska; 20,320 ft.
Madeira, river, Brazil; flows into Amazon
Madhya Pradesh, state, India; cap. Bhopal
Madinat ash Sha'b, town and cap. of People's Dem.
   Rep. of Yemen
Madison, cap. of Wisconsin, W. of Milwaukee
Madras, city, port and cap. of Tamil Nadu state,
   India
Madrid, cap. of Spain, on Manzanares River
Maharashtra, state, India; cap. Bombay
Maine, N.E. state of U.S.A.; cap. Augusta
Maipo, mt., Argentina
Makalu, Mt., Tibet/Nepal; 27,790 ft.
Malagasy Rep., state, Indian Ocean
Malawi, rep., central Africa
Malaya, states, W. Malaysia; southern part of Malay
   Pen.; cap. Kuala Lumpur

Malaysia, federation, S.E. Asia
Maldive Islands, Indian Ocean, S.W. of Ceylon
Mali, rep., cent. Africa; cap. Bamako
Malta, island and state, in cent. Mediterranean; cap. Valletta
Man, Isle of, Irish Sea; cap. Douglas
Managua, town and cap. of Nicaragua
Manchester, city, Lancashire, England
Manila, port, Luzon I., Philippines
Manitoba, prov., Canada; cap. Winnipeg
Maranhão, state, Brazil
Marseilles, port, France, S. coast
Martinique, French island, W. Indies
Maryland, Atlantic state of U.S.A.; cap. Annapolis
Maseru City, cap. of Lesotho
Massachusetts, state, U.S.A.; cap. Boston
Mato Grosso, state, Brazil
Matterhorn, alpine peak, Switzerland; 14,705 ft.
Mauritius, state and I., Indian Ocean
Mauritania, rep., W. Africa; cap. Nouakchott
Meghalaya, state, N.E. India
Mekong, river, S.E. Asia; length 2,750 miles
Melbourne, cap. of Victoria, Australia
Melilla, port and settlement, N. coast of Morocco
Memphis, town, Tennessee, on Mississippi
Mexico, state, N. America
Mexico City, cap. of the rep. of Mexico, N. America
Miami, city and winter resort, Florida
Michigan, state of U.S.A.; capital Lansing
Michigan, Lake, N. America
Milan, city, Lombardy, N. Italy
Milwaukee, city and port, Wisconsin
Minas Gerais, state, Brazil

Minneapolis, city, Minnesota, on Mississippi

Minnesota, north-central state, U.S.A.; cap. St Paul

Minsk, cap. of Byelorussia, U.S.S.R.

Miquelon, island, off S.W. Newfoundland

Mississippi, great river of U.S.A., flows to G. of Mexico; length 3160 miles

Mississippi, state of U.S.A.; cap. Jackson

Missouri, state, U.S.A.; cap. Jefferson City

Missouri, river, 3000 m. long; joins Mississippi

Mobile, port city, Alabama

Mogadishu (Mogadiscio), town and cap. of Somali Rep.

Moldavia, rep., U.S.S.R. in S.W.

Monaco, small principality and town, on Mediterranean Riviera

Mongolia, rep., central Asia; cap. Ulan Bator

Monmouth, co., Wales

Monrovia, cap. of Liberia, W. Africa

Montana, N.W. state of U.S.A.; cap. Helena

Mont Blanc, France-Italy, highest peak of Alps; 15,772 ft.

Montevideo, cap. and chief port, Uruguay

Montgomery, cap. of Alabama, U.S.A.

Montreal, city, Quebec, E.N.E. of Ottawa

Montserrat, island, Leeward Is., W. Indies

Morocco, kingdom, N.W. Africa; caps. Rabat and Tangier

Moscow (Moskva), prov. and cap. of the R.S.F.S.R.

Mozambique (Moçambique), Portuguese province, E. Africa; cap. Lourenço Marques

Mulhacen, mt., Spain

Munich (München), cy., W. Germany, on R. Isar

Muscat, cap. of Oman, Arabia, on G. of Oman

Mysore, state and town, South India; cap. Bangalore

Nagaland, state of N.E. India
Nagoya, town, Honshu I., Japan
Naha, town and cap. of Ryukyu Is.
Nairobi, cap. of Kenya, East Africa
Namibia=South West Africa
Nanda Devi, mt., Himalayas, Uttar Pradesh
Nanga Parbat, mt., Kashmir; 26,620 ft.
Nanking, city, China, on the Yangtze Kiang
Naples, city and naval base, Italy, S.E. of Rome
Nashville, cap. of Tennessee, on Cumberland R.
Nassau, cap. of Bahamas, New Providence I.
Natal, prov., S. Africa; cap. Pietermaritzburg
Nauru Island, Pacific, N.E. of Solomon Islands
Nebraska, state, U.S.A.; cap. Lincoln
Nepal, independent state, in the Himalayas
Netherlands, kingdom, W. Europe; caps. Amsterdam
  and The Hague
Nevada, west. state, U.S.A.: cap. Carson City
Nevis, I., Leeward Is., W. Indies
Newark, city, New Jersey, N.W. of Staten I.
New Bedford, town, Massachusetts
New Brunswick, E. maritime prov. of Canada
New Caledonia, French island, in S. Pacific
Newcastle, port, New South Wales, N. of Sydney
Newcastle upon Tyne, city and port, Northumberland,
  England
Newfoundland, island and prov. of E. Canada; cap. St
  John's
New Guinea, island in W. Pacific
New Hampshire, New England state, U.S.A.; cap.
  Concord
New Haven, port, Connecticut, N.E. of N.Y.
New Hebrides, island group, W. Pacific

New Jersey, a New England state of U.S.A.; cap. Trenton

New Mexico, state, U.S.A.; cap. Santa Fé

New Orleans, port and cap. of Louisiana

Newport, tn. and port, Monmouthshire, Wales

Newport News, port, Virginia, N.W. of Norfolk

New South Wales, state, Aust.; cap. Sydney

New York, state, U.S.A.; cap. Albany

New York, city and port, U.S.A.

New Zealand, state, S. Pacific; cap. Wellington

Niagara Falls, city, New York, at falls of Niagara river

Niamey, town and cap. of Niger, West Africa

Nicaragua, rep., Cent. America; cap. Managua

Nicaragua, Lake, S. America

Nicosia, cap. of Cyprus, Mediterranean

Niger, river, W. Africa, flows 2600 m. to G. of Guinea

Niger, republic, W. Africa; cap. Niamey

Nigeria, rep., West Africa; cap. Lagos

Nile, river, N.E. Africa, flows 3600 miles to Mediterranean

Ningsia-Hui, aut. reg., China

Niue, island, one of Cook Is.

Norfolk, city, port and naval base, Virginia

Norfolk Island, Pacific Oc., N.N.W. of N.Z.

Northampton, co. town, Northants, England

North Carolina, state, U.S.A.; cap. Raleigh

North Dakota, a N. central state, U.S.A.; cap. Bismarck

Northern Ireland, prov., U.K.

Northern Territory, territory, Australia; cap. Darwin

Northwest Territories, prov., Canada

Norway, kingdom, Scandinavia, W. Europe; cap. Oslo

Norwich, town, Norfolk, England

Nottingham, co. town of Notts, England

Nouakchott, cap. of Mauritania, W. Africa
Nova Scotia, E. maritime prov., Canada; cap. Halifax
Novosibirsk, town, on Ob river, U.S.S.R., E. of Omsk
Nyasa, Lake, S.E. Africa
Oakland, city, California, on San Francisco B.
Ob, river, U.S.S.R., flows 2420 m. to Arctic Oc.
Odessa, city and port, Ukraine, on Black Sea
Ohio, state, U.S.A.; cap. Columbus
Oklahoma, state, U.S.A. cap. Oklahoma City
Oklahoma City, cap. of Oklahoma state, U.S.A.
Oldham, town, Lancashire, England
Omaha, city & riv. port, Nebraska, on Missouri
Omsk, town, U.S.S.R., S.E. of Sverdlovsk
Onega, Lake, U.S.S.R., E. of Lake Ladoga
Ontario, E., province, Canada; cap. Toronto
Ontario, Lake, between Canada and U.S.A.
Oporto, city, Portugal, on the Douro
Orange Free State, prov., S. Africa; cap. Bloemfontein
Oregon, N.W. state of U.S.A.; cap. Salem
Orissa, state, India; cap. Bhubaneswar
Osaka, city and port, Honshu, Japan
Oslo, city and cap. of Norway, on Oslo Fjord
Ottawa, cap. of Canada, on Ottawa riv., Ontario
Ouagadougou, town and cap. of Upper Volta
Oxford, univ. and co. town of Oxfordshire, England
Pakistan, state, S. Asia; cap. Islamabad
Palermo, port and cap. of Sicily
Panama City, port & cap. of the rep. of Panama
Panama, republic, cent. America
Papua, S.E. part of the island of New Guinea; cap. **Port** Moresby
Para, state, Brazil
Paraguay, republic, S. America; cap. Asuncion

Paraíba, state, Brazil
Paramaribo, cap. of Surinam, S. America
Paraná, state, Brazil
Paraná, river, Brazil
Paris, cap. of France, on the River Seine
Pasadena, town, California
Paterson, city, New Jersey, N.W. of New York
Peking, city, Hopeh prov., cap. of China
Pennsylvania, state, U.S.A., cap. Harrisburg
Peoria, city, Illinois, S.W. of Chicago
Perm, town, U.S.S.R., on river Kama
Pernambuco, state, Brazil
Perth, cap. of W. Australia, S.W. coast
Peru, rep., S. America
Philadelphia, city, Pennsyl., S.W. of New York
Philippines, ils., rep. E. Indies, cap. Manilla
Phnom Penh, cap. of Cambodia, Indo-China
Phœnix, cap. of Arizona, N.E. of Tucson
Phœnix Islands, group, N.E. of Fiji, Pacific Oc.
Piaul, state, Brazil
Pietermaritzburg, cap. of Natal, S. Africa
Pitcairn Island, E. Pacific, S.E. of Tuamotu Archipelago
Pittsburgh, city, Pennsylvania
Plymouth, port, Devon, England
Poland, rep., central Europe ; cap. Warsaw
Popocatepetl ("smoking mountain"), Mexico, S.E. of
    Mexico, height 17,887 ft.
Port-au-Prince, cap. and chief port, Haiti
Port Elizabeth, port, on Algoa B., Cape Prov.
Portland, city, Oregon, on Williamette river
Port Louis, town and cap. of Mauritius
Port of Spain, cap. of Trinidad, W. Indies
Porto Novo, cap. of Dahomey, W. Africa

Portsmouth, city, port and naval base, Hants, England
Portsmouth, town, Virginia
Portugal, republic, S.W. Europe, cap. Lisbon
Portuguese Guinea, colony, W. Africa; cap. Bissau
Prague (Praha), city, Bohemia, cap. of Czechoslovakia
Preston, town, Lancs, England, N.E. of Liverpool
Pretoria, town and cap. of S. Africa
Prince Edward Island, prov., Canada; cap. Charlotte-town
Principe, Portuguese island, in G. of Guinea, W. Africa
Providence, city & cap. of Rhode Is., U.S.A.
Puerto Rico, Is., Greater Antilles, W. Indies
Punjab, state, N.W. India
Pusan, port, S. Korea
Pyongyang, city and cap. of N. Korea
Qatar, sheikdom, Arabia, in Persian Gulf
Quebec, tn. and cap. of Quebec prov., Canada
Quebec, prov., Canada
Queensland, state, Australia; cap. Brisbane
Quezon City, cap. of the Philippines
Quito, city, cap. of Ecuador, S. America
R.S.F.S.R.= Russian Soviet Federated Socialist Republic
Rabat, tn. & cap. of Morocco, S.W. of Tangier
Rajasthan, state, N.W. India; cap. Jaipur
Rangoon, city and port; cap. of Burma
Rawalpindi, dist. and town, W. Pakistan
Reading, town, Berkshire, England
Recife, city, Brazil, N.E. Brazil
Regina, cap. of Saskatchewan, W. of Winnipeg
Réunion, I., Indian Ocean
Reykjavik, cap. of Iceland, on S.W. coast
Rhode Island, New England state, U.S.A.; cap. Providence

Rhodesia, state, central Africa, cap. Salisbury
Richmond, cap. of Virginia, U.S.A.
Riga, port and cap. of Latvia, on G. of Riga
Rio de Janeiro, city, Brazil
Rio de Janeiro, state; Brazil
Rio del Norte, river, Brazil
Rio Grande do Norte, state, Brazil
Rio Grande do Sul, state, Brazil
Riyadh, Najd, cap. of Saudi Arabia
Robson, Mt., Brit. Columbia
Rochester, city, New York, near L. Ontario
Rockford, town, Illinois
Rome (Roma), city, cap. of Italy, on River Tiber
Romania, rep., S.E. Europe, cap. Bucharest
Rondônia, state, Brazil
Roraima, state, Brazil
Rosa, Monte, Pennine Alps, Switzerland and Italy,
    height 15,216 ft.
Rostov, town, U.S.S.R., at mouth of the Don
Rotterdam, cy. & pt., Netherlands, on R. Maas
Russia= R.S.F.S.R.
Ruwenzori, Mt., Congo/Uganda; 16,794 ft.
Rwanda, republic, central Africa, cap. Kigali
Ryukyu Archipelago, chain of Is., from Japan to Formosa
Sabah (North Borneo), state, E. Malaysia, cap.
    Jesselton
Sacramento, city and cap. of California
Saigon, port and cap. of S. Vietnam
St Christopher= St Kitts
St Helena, island, S. Atlantic Ocean
St Helens, town, Lancs, Eng., near Liverpool
St John, town and port, New Brunswick
St John's, town & port, cap. of Newfoundland

St Kitts, island, Leeward Is., W. Indies
St Lawrence, great riv. of N. America ; 2340 m.
St Louis, city, Missouri, on the Mississippi
St Lucia, island, Windward group, W. Indies
St Paul, city, Minnesota, on Mississippi
St Petersburg, town, Florida
St Pierre, island, Atlantic, S. of Newfoundland
St Vincent, island, Windward Is., W. Indies
Salford, town, Lancs., England
Salisbury, cap. of Rhodesia, central Africa
Salt Lake City, cap. of Utah, on River Jordan
Salvador, El, rep., Cent. Amer. ; cap. San Salvador
San'a, cap. of Yemen, Arabia
San Antonio, city, Texas, W. of Houston
San Diego, city and naval base, California
San Francisco, city and port, California
San José, city and cap. of Costa Rica
San Jose, town, California
San Juan, cap. of Puerto Rico, W. Indies
San Marino, rep., N.E. Italy
San Salvador, cap. of El Salvador, Cent. America
Santa Ana, town, California
Santa Caterina, state, Brazil
Santiago, city, cap. of Chile, S. America
Santo Domingo, town and cap. of Dominican Rep.,
   West Indies
São Francisco, river, Brazil
São Paulo, city, Brazil, N.W. of Santos
São Paulo, state, Brazil
São Tomé, island in G. of Guinea, W. Africa
Saratov, town, U.S.S.R., S.E. of Moscow
Sarawak, state, E. Malaysia
Saskatchewan, W. prov. of Canada ; cap. Regina

Saskatoon, town, Saskatchewan, N.W. of Regina
Saudi Arabia, kingdom, S.W. Asia; cap. Riyadh
Savannah, port, Georgia, U.S.A.
Scotland, northern part of Great Britain; kingdom, cap.
  Edinburgh
Scranton, city, Pennsyl., N.W. of Philadelphia
Seattle, port, Washington, on Puget Sound
Senegal, republic and river, N.W. Africa; cap. Dakar
Seoul (Kyongsong), city and cap. of S. Korea
Sergipe, state, Brazil
Seychelles, Is., Indian Ocean
Shanghai, port, Kiangsu prov., China
Shansi, prov., China
Shantung, prov., China
Sheffield, city, Yorks, England
Shensi, prov., China
Shenyang (Moukden), city, N.E. China
Shreveport, town, Louisiana, U.S.A.
Sian (Changan), cap. of Shensi prov., China·
Sierra Leone, rep., W. Africa; cap. Freetown
Sikkim, state, N.E. India; cap. Gangtok
Singapore, island,.rep., port and naval base, S. of Malaya
Sinkiang-Uighur, aut. reg., W. China; cap. Urumchi
Slave Lake, Great, N.W. Territories, Canada
Sofia, city, cap. of Bulgaria
Solihull, town, Warks., England
Solomon Islands, Melanesia, Pacific Ocean
Somali Republic, state, E. Africa; cap. Mogadishu
Southampton, port, Hampshire, England
South Africa, rep., cap. Pretoria
South Australia, state, Aust.; cap. Adelaide
South Bend, town, Indiana, E. of Chicago
South Carolina, state, U.S.A.; cap. Columbia

South Dakota, state, U.S.A.; cap. Pierre
Southend-on-Sea, seaside resort, Essex, England
South Shields, port, Durham, England
South West Africa (Namibia), state, S. Africa
Spain, state, S.W. Europe; cap. Madrid
Spanish Sahara, prov., W. Africa
Spitsbergen, islands, Arctic Oc., N. of Norway
Spokane, town, Washington, N.E. of Portland
Springfield, town, Massachusetts, S.W. of Boston
Springs, town, S. Africa
Stanley, port and cap. of Falkland Is.
Stewart Island, to south of South I., N.Z.
Stockholm, port, and cap. of Sweden
Stockport, town, Cheshire, England
Stoke-on-Trent, city, Staffs, England
Stuttgart, city, W. Germany
Sucre, town and cap. of Bolivia
Sudan, rep., N.E. Africa; cap. Khartoum
Sudbury, town, Ontario, N.W. of Montreal
Sunderland, port, Durham, England
Superior, L., Canada and U.S.A.; length 360 m.
Surabaja, port, Java, Indonesia
Surinam, prov. of Netherlands, S. America
Svalbard, arch., Arctic Ocean
Sverdlovsk, town, in Ural Mts., U.S.S.R.
Swansea, port, Glamorganshire, Wales
Swaziland, kingdom, S. Africa
Sweden, kingdom, Scandinavia, W. Europe; cap.
  Stockholm
Switzerland, rep., central Europe, cap. Berne
Sydney, city, cap. of New South Wales
Syracuse, town, New York, E. of Rochester
Syria, rep., W. Asia; cap. Damascus

Szechwan, prov., China
Tacoma, town, Washington, N.E. of Olympia
Tadzhikistan, rep., U.S.S.R.; cap. Dushanbe
Taipei, town and cap. of Taiwan
Taiwan (Formosa), island and rep., to E. of China
Taiyuan (Yangku), city, Shansi prov., China
Ta'izz, town, Yemen
Tamil Nadu, state, S.E. India, cap. Madras
Tampa, town, Florida, on Tampa Bay
Tananarive, cap. of Malagasy Rep.
Tanganyika, Lake, E. Africa
Tanzania, rep., E. Africa, cap. Dar es Salaam
Tashkent, city, cap. of Uzbekistan, N.E. of Samarkand
Tasman, Mt., N.Z.
Tasmania, island state, Commonwealth of Aust.
Tbilisi, cap. of Georgian rep., U.S.S.R.
Teesside, town, England, S. of Newcastle
Tegucigalpa, cap. of Honduras, Cent. America
Tehran, cap. of Iran, S. of Caspian Sea
Tennessee, state, U.S.A.; cap. Nashville
Texas, a southern state of U.S.A.; cap. Austin
Thailand (Siam), kingdom, S.E. Asia; cap. Bangkok
Thimphu, town and cap. of Bhutan
Tibet, aut. reg., W. China; cap. Lhasa
Tientsin, port, Hopeh, China, S.E. of Peking
Timor, prov., Indonesia, S.E. of Celébes
Tinguiririca, Mt., Chile
Tiranë, cap. of Albania, Europe
Titicaca, Lake, Peru and Bolivia, in the Andes
Tobago, island, Trinidad and Tobago
Togo, rep., W. Africa, cap. Lomé
Tokelau Is., group, Pacific Ocean

Tokyo, city and cap. of Japan, Honshu I.
Toledo, town, Ohio, W. of Cleveland
Tolima, mt., Colombia
Tonga Islands, Polynesia, Pacific Ocean
Topeka, city, cap. of Kansas, U.S.A.
Torbay, town, Devon, England
Toronto, city, cap. of Ontario, Canada
Torrance, town, California
Transvaal, prov., S. Africa; cap. Pretoria
Trenton, city and cap. of New Jersey
Trinidad, island, W. Indies, part of rep. of Trinidad and Tobago; cap. Port of Spain
Tripoli, port and naval base, Libya
Tristan da Cunha, volcanic island, S. Atlantic Oc.
Tsingtao, port, Shantung, on Kiaochow Bay
Tucson, town, Arizona, S.E. of Phoenix
Tulsa, town, Oklahoma
Tunis, town and cap. of Tunisia
Tunisia, rep., North Africa; cap. Tunis
Tupungato, mt., S. America
Turin, town, Piedmont, N. Italy
Turkey, rep., Europe and Asia; cap. Ankara
Turkmenistan, rep., U.S.S.R.; cap. Ashkhabad
Turks Islands, group of islands, S. of the Bahamas
U.A.R.= United Arab Republic
U.K.= United Kingdom of Great Britain and Northern Ireland
U.S.A.= United States of America
U.S.S.R.= Union of Soviet Socialist Republics
Ufa, town, U.S.S.R., S.W. of Sverdlovsk
Uganda, state, Africa; cap. Entebbe
Ukraine, rep., U.S.S.R.; cap. Kiev (Kiyev)
Ulan Bator, town and cap. of Mongolia

Union of Soviet Socialist Republics, state, Europe and Asia; cap. Moscow

United Arab Republic (Egypt), Africa; cap. Cairo

United Kingdom of Great Britain and Northern Ireland, state, W. Europe; cap. London

United States of America, state, N. America; cap. Washington

Upper Volta, rep., W. Africa; cap. Ouagadougou

Uruguay, rep. and river, S. America; length 950 m. cap. Montevideo

Utah, inland state, U.S.A.; cap. Salt Lake City

Uttar Pradesh, state, India; chief tn. Lucknow

Utica, town, New York, N.W. of Albany

Uzbekistan, rep., U.S.S.R.; cap. Tashkent

Vaduz, cap. of the principality of Liechtenstein

Valencia, port, Spain, on east coast

Valletta, port and cap. of Malta

Vancouver, city, Brit. Columbia, N. of Victoria

Vänern, lake, SW Sweden; length 95 m.

Venezuela, rep., S. America; cap. Caracas

Vermont, a New England state, U.S.A.; cap. Montpelier

Vesuvius, Mount, vol., Italy, on B. of Naples

Victoria, state, S.E. Aust.; cap. Melbourne

Victoria, cap. of Br. Columbia, on Vancouver I.

Victoria, cap. and chief port, Hong Kong

Victoria, Lake, Africa, between Uganda, Tanzania and Kenya

Vienna (Wien), city, cap. of Austria, on Danube

Vientiane, town and cap. of Laos, on Mekong R.

Vietnam, N. and S., reps., S.E. Asia

Virgin Islands, group in West Indies

Virginia, a S. Atlantic state, U.S.A.; **cap. Richmond**

Volga, river, U.S.S.R., falls into Caspian Sea; length 2320 m.
Volgograd, town, U.S.S.R., N.W. of Astrakhan
Voronezh, town, U.S.S.R., S.S.E. of Moscow
Wales, principality, W. of England
Walsall, town, Staffs., England
Wallasey, town, Ches., England
Warley, town, Worcs, England
Warsaw (Warszawa), cap. of Poland, on the River Vistula
Washington, city, Dist. of Columbia; cap. of United States
Washington, Pacific state, U.S.A.; cap. Olympia
Waterbury, town, Connecticut
Wellington, city and cap. of New Zealand, on North Island
Western Australia, state, Aust.; cap. Perth
West Bengal, state, India
West Bromwich, town, Staffs., England
Western Samoa, state, Pacific Ocean; cap. Apia
West Virginia, state, U.S.A.; cap. Charleston
Whitney, Mt., California
Wichita, town, Kansas, on Arkansas River
Wichita Falls, town, Texas
Windsor, port, Ontario, Canada
Windward Islands, part of the Lesser Antilles
Winnipeg, city, cap. of Manitoba, Canada
Winnipeg, Lake, Canada
Winston Salem, town, N. Carolina
Wisconsin, state, U.S.A.; cap. Madison
Wollongong, port, New South Wales, S. of Sydney
Wolverhampton, town, Staffordshire, England
Worcester, town, Mass., W.S.W. of Boston

Wuhan (Hankow), river port, China, on Yangtze Kiang, in Hupeh prov.

Wyoming, N.W. state, U.S.A.; cap. Cheyenne

Yangtze Kiang, river, China, rises in Tibet; length 3000 m.

Yaoundé, cap. of Cameroun, Africa

Yemen, rep., S.W. Arabia; cap. San'a

Yemen, People's Dem. Rep. of, S. Arabia; cap. ash Sha'b

Yenisey, river, U.S.S.R., flows to Arctic Sea

Yerevan, town and cap. of Armenia

Yokohama, port, Japan, Honshu Island

Yonkers, town, New York

York, city and co. town of Yorkshire, England

Youngstown, town, Ohio

Yugoslavia, republic, S.E. Europe, in Balkans; cap. Belgrade

Yukon, river, Yukon and Alaska, flows S.W. to the Bering Sea

Yukon, territory, N.W. Canada; cap. Dawson

Yunnan, prov., China

Zagreb, town, Croatia, Yugoslavia, on R. Sava

Zambezi, river, S. Africa, flows 1600 m. into the Indian Ocean

Zambia, republic, central Africa; cap. Lusaka

Zanzibar, island & town, Tanzania

Zaporozh'ye, town, Ukraine, W.S.W. of Donetsk

Zomba, town and cap. of Malawi